D0599634

THE COMPLETE BOOK OF

DRIED- FLOWER TOPIARIES

THE COMPLETE BOOK OF

DRIED-

FLOWER

TOPIARIES

A STEP-BY-STEP GUIDE TO CREATING 25 STUNNING ARRANGEMENTS

CAROL ENDLER STERBENZ
PHOTOGRAPHY BY RICHARD FELBER

RUNNING PRESS
PHILADELPHIA · LONDON

Copyright © 1995 by Carol Endler Sterbenz

All rights reserved under the Pan-American and International Copyright Conventions.
This book may not be reproduced in whole or in part, in any form or by any means,
electronic or mechanical, including photocopying, recording, or by any
information storage and retrieval system now known or hereafter
invented, without written permission from the publisher.

9 8 7 6 5 4 3 2 1

Digit on the right indicates the number of this printing.

Library of Congress Cataloging-in-Publication Number 94-73887
ISBN 1-56138-451-8

THE COMPLETE BOOK OF DRIED-FLOWER TOPIARIES
A Step-by-Step Guide to Creating 25 Stunning Arrangements
was prepared and produced by
Michael Friedman Publishing Group, Inc.
15 West 26th Street
New York, New York 10010

Editor: Elizabeth Viscott Sullivan
Directions Editor: Kathleen Berlew
Art Director: Jeff Batzli
Designer: Susan E. Livingston
Photography Director: Christopher C. Bain
Props and Styling: Sylvia Lachter
Photography © Richard Felber

Color separation by Bright Arts (Singapore) Pte. Ltd.
Printed in China by Leefung-Asco Printers Ltd.

This book may be ordered by mail from the publisher.
Please add $2.50 for postage and handling.
But try your bookstore first!

Running Press Book Publishers
125 South Twenty-second Street
Philadelphia, Pennsylvania 19103-4399

For George, Bert, and Gus

CONTENTS

INTRODUCTION
8

PART I
TOPIARY-MAKING BASICS

PART II
THE TOPIARY COLLECTION

APPENDICES

INTRODUCTION

Making a dried-flower topiary is one of the most satisfying ways to work with dried flowers and foliage. Whether shaped into domes in pretty pots, globes with stems, patchwork patterns in low boxes, or any one of the vast number of variations possible, dried-flower topiaries are easily produced by experienced and novice crafters alike. All of the necessary tools and materials are readily available, and you probably own many of them already. Best of all, the construction techniques are simple to learn and can be used to make topiaries of any size, complexity, or design.

Of course, using dried flowers and foliage to create decorative accents is nothing new. Dried flowers have always been fashionable, most notably since the Victorian era, when small bouquets, known as tussie-mussies, graced side tables, providing rooms with attractive visual accents.

Dried flowers are popular choices for floral decoration for several reasons: they extend the decorative life of certain flowers; they emphasize the intrinsic beauty of flowers in their dried form; and they can be displayed year-round.

Today, dried flowers are arranged into virtually every shape and placed in every decorative vessel imaginable, from circular wreaths of velvety cockscomb to Lalique vases filled with majestic spires of larkspur and pussy willows. Add to design possibilities the noble topiary, historically related to the aristocratic hedge gardens so popular in the sixteenth and seventeenth centuries, and you have a unique and striking application of dried-flower arranging that produces fabulous, eye-catching results.

The Complete Book of Dried-Flower Topiaries was written to make the art of topiary making accessible. All the techniques are demonstrated here, and these techniques form the basis for the collection of projects included in the chapters that follow. Once you have mastered the basic styles—the dome, the globe, and the standard—you will be able to make virtually any topiary. Look at this book as your handbook to dried-flower topiaries; its step-by-step instructions will lead you through the whole process. In no time at all, you will begin to understand the capabilities of dried flowers, and hopefully, you will be inspired to use your favorite flowers in innovative topiaries of your own design.

Part One

TOPIARY-MAKING BASICS

Chapter 1

TOOLS
AND
MATERIALS

TOOLS

Even the most modestly stocked tool kit or kitchen utensil drawer probably houses most of the tools essential to making any topiary in this book. These tools perform a few select but critical functions; they must either cut, bend, or join the materials used to construct or decorate the topiary.

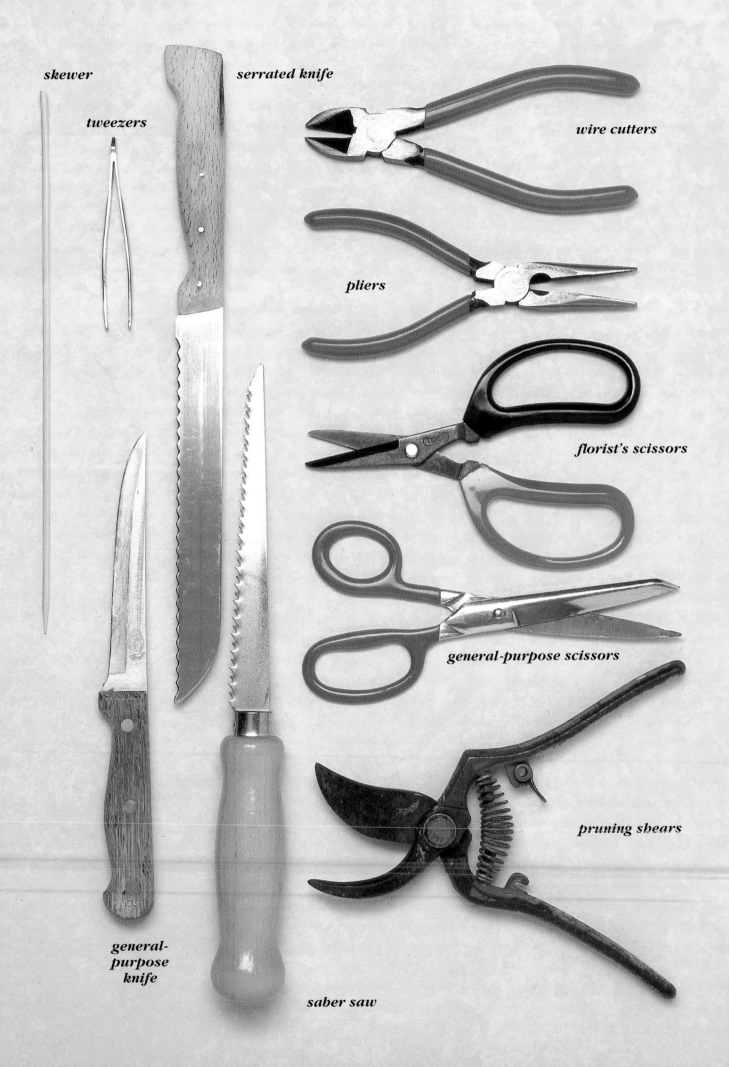

skewer

tweezers

serrated knife

wire cutters

pliers

florist's scissors

general-purpose scissors

pruning shears

general-
purpose
knife

saber saw

The essential cutting tools are general-purpose scissors, a sharp general-purpose knife, and a saber saw. Florist's scissors, pruning shears, wire cutters, and a serrated knife will facilitate the cutting tasks, and are designed to give you more refined results. The second task—that of bending and gripping materials, which will most often be wire products—can be performed with one pair of all-purpose narrow-nosed pliers. Tweezers can be helpful for picking up small, fragile flowers.

The making of any topiary is divided into three stages: the preparation of the materials, the construction of the basic parts of the topiary, and the decoration of the topiary. All tools can be used in any stage of the creation process as long as they do the job properly. For example, the scissors you use in preparing the dried material can also be used in cutting flower stems in the decorating stage.

With some exception, substituting one tool for another is fine as long as the tool is capable of accomplishing the task. Scissors are usually not used on wire, especially medium- and heavy-gauge wire, which can pit or misalign the blades. But general-purpose scissors will cut fine-gauge wire easily without ruining the blades. Pliers that have a straight section close to the joint for cutting wire can double for wire cutters. Of course, some tools are best suited to their original purpose, and using them as intended will minimize mistakes and maximize efforts.

Familiarize yourself with the universe of tools. As you become more adept at topiary making, you will demand tools that create the desired results quickly and easily.

To follow is a description of each tool used in this book. This list will guide you in collecting a set of tools that will enable you to make any topiary featured in or inspired by this collection.

GENERAL-PURPOSE SCISSORS

General-purpose scissors are a good cutting tool for light- to medium-weight materials such as paper, ribbon, thin wire, and thin-stemmed foliage and flowers. The blades should be kept dry to prevent rusting.

GENERAL-PURPOSE KNIFE

Any sharp knife, such as an old steak knife or paring knife, that is maneuverable enough to slice, carve, and pare natural materials will serve the purpose. The knife's handle should fit comfortably in your hand so that it can be easily manipulated.

When sculpting dry foam, hold the knife in your hand with your thumb on the blunt top edge of the blade. Then lay the blade on an angle on the foam and turn your wrist toward your body, cutting shapes from the foam in a scooping motion.

You can use an emery stone to sharpen the blade as needed.

FLORIST'S SCISSORS

A most useful tool, florist's scissors cut precisely and cleanly, are excellent for snipping fragile, slender stems, and their short, very sharp blades won't grind the floral material as general-purpose scissors might. Florist's scissors should not be used for thick woody material, cardboard, or metals that will dent or misalign the blades. The handles are often coated with colored plastic, which makes the scissors easier to identify and grip. Dry the blades after each use in order to prevent rusting.

Pruning Shears

Pruning shears have short handles and heavy-duty jaws that cut through medium-thick woody stems and branches easily. The spring-action handles require a firm hold and a relatively wide one-handed grip. (Two hands may be required for heavier cutting.)

Pruning shears can usually accommodate material with a diameter of $\frac{1}{2}$ inch (1.3cm) or so. To cut branches larger than $\frac{1}{2}$-inch (1.3cm) thickness, rock the clenched jaws of the pruning shears back and forth to break the plant fiber a little at a time. (Cut away any stringy edges that result with general-purpose scissors or a sharp saw.) For branches of harder woods like oak and maple, a sharp saw may be required for a clean cut.

Wire Cutters

Wire cutters have strong, angled jaws that crimp and cut through most gauges of wire, including chicken wire. To use, hold the handles in one hand and clench the jaws on the wire at the point where you want the cut, then squeeze the handles firmly. The jaws will snap a clean cut on thin wire with very little pressure. For thicker wire, rock the clenched jaws of the wire cutters back and forth, then cut through the groove that forms. Steel wire cutters tend to last longer than other types.

Saber Saw

A saber saw will cut through medium- and heavy-weight stems and branches, but it is primarily used for making large cuts in dry-foam blocks, sheets, and other shapes. The saw's short blade makes it easy to control, therefore the length of cuts can be planned and curved cuts accomplished. The saber saw's high (3–4mm), widely spaced (2mm) teeth easily cut dry foam, especially Styrofoam. Because plastic dust results from the tearing action of the blade, you should wear a mask and work in a ventilated area.

Serrated Knife

The serrated knife is highly effective in sculpting and making straight cuts through all florist's foam, especially dry foam (Oasis). The blade of the serrated knife is slender and flat; its wavy cutting edge grips the dry foam, making even, clean cuts. It is sharp enough to shave very thin slices from a larger section of dry foam. To make a straight clean cut, lay the knife perpendicular to the dry foam and push it down with light pressure (do not use a sawing motion).

Pliers

Pliers are used for clasping and articulating wire so that it can be bent into a particular shape, and for holding and positioning small material. Because pliers usually have a long nose and flat interior jaw surface, they are useful for holding any wire or stemmed plant material.

To bend a narrow U-shaped end in a wire (used in making false stems), pinch the end of the wire between the narrowest part of the jaws and rotate the nose of the pliers 45 degrees to 90 degrees in one direction to curve the wire around one jaw. To create a small hoop, continue turning the nose of the pliers 360 degrees.

Pliers are also useful for gripping any material that is difficult to hold due to its position, texture, or temperature. Remember: pliers will conduct heat. Use pot holders when lifting or bending heated materials with the pliers.

TWEEZERS

Tweezers are not essential when constructing a topiary, but they can be indispensable when decorating one. Ideal for picking up and holding small stems and petals, tweezers are especially useful in the repair of dried-flower arrangements (see page 116).

Use cosmetic tweezers with a broad nose instead of needle-nosed tweezers, as the latter could accidentally pierce the dried material.

SKEWERS

Skewers are useful for positioning materials—in hot glue, for example—or for making holes in soft materials. Because skewers usually have a very sharp tip on each end, they can also be used for picking floral material—adding a main stem to one or more stems so that they can be inserted into a base material (see "Making Your Own Florist's Picks" on page 36).

MATERIALS

There are three types of craft materials used in the making of any topiary: the material that comprises the head of the topiary, such as foam forms; the materials that fill or stabilize the topiary container; and the materials used to connect and secure the parts of the topiary and its decoration. These materials, which are few but specific, are available at craft, hardware, or garden supply stores.

The basic head of any topiary is usually made from soft material such as dry foam. The foam is easy to pierce and is commonly available in a variety of sizes, shapes, and types. The adhesives used include white glue, hot glue, and tape. Binding materials such as wire, florist's staples, and florist's picks facilitate the attaching of decorative material to the already-constructed topiary.

The text to follow summarizes the characteristics and use of each of the materials that can be employed to construct and decorate a topiary. Many materials are interchangeable—such as adhesive clay (florist's clay tape) and hot glue, if the project calls for simple adhesion. However, when a more complex construction is being made, stronger adhesion such as that offered by packing tape is more desirable. Familiarize yourself with each of these materials so that you can choose the appropriate item.

STEM WRAP

Stem wrap is a nonsticky, flexible tape with adhesive properties. It is used to bundle stems together and to conceal stems that have been reinforced with wire.

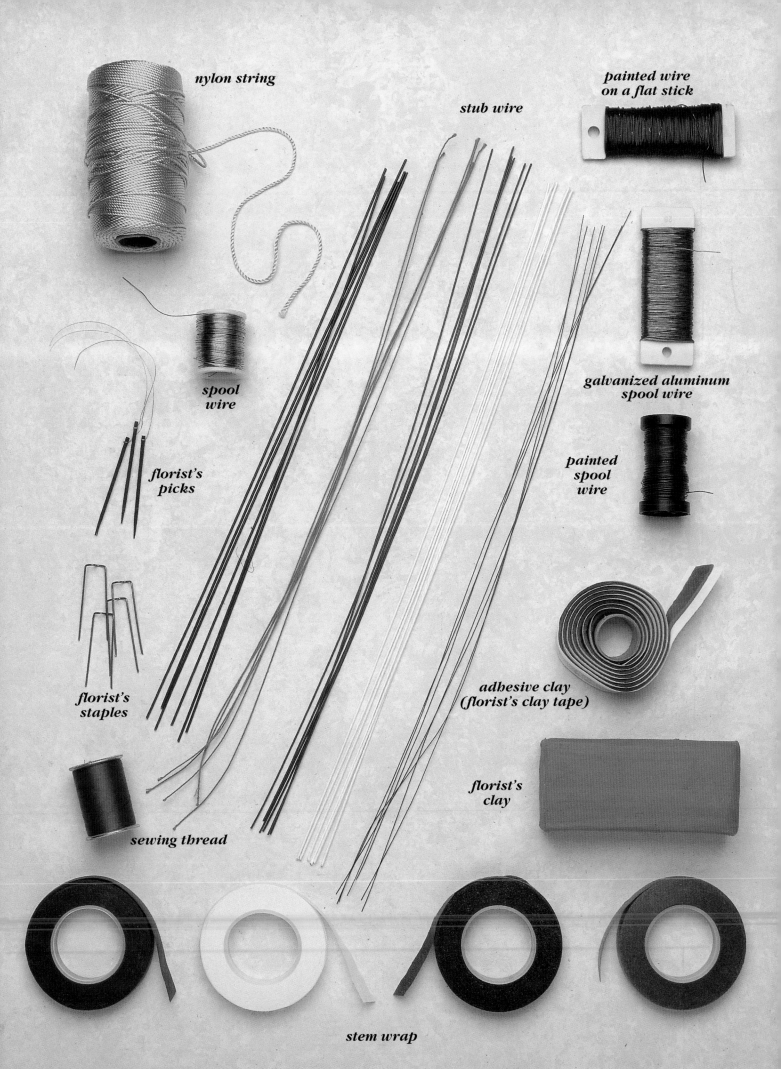

nylon string

painted wire
on a flat stick

stub wire

spool
wire

galvanized aluminum
spool wire

painted
spool
wire

florist's
picks

florist's
staples

adhesive clay
(florist's clay tape)

florist's
clay

sewing thread

stem wrap

WIRE

One of the most frequently used binding materials, wire is available in precut lengths (called stub wire), and is wound on flat sticks and spools. Wire thickness is indicated by gauge; the higher the gauge number, the finer (or thinner) the wire.

Thin wire is suited to making false stems for fragile-stemmed material and for hanging lightweight materials for drying. Very fine wire on a spool is often referred to as rose wire; this type of wire is most often available in galvanized aluminum. Medium-gauge wire is frequently used to reinforce fragile stems and create false stems. It is available in unpainted, painted, and cotton-wrapped varieties, in precut lengths and on spools. Heavy-gauge wire is almost always found on spools. It is used for reinforcing the trunks of topiaries or for binding together heavier materials for large arrangements.

FLORIST'S STAPLES

Florist's staples are horseshoe-shaped wires used for anchoring dried material to the base material (usually foam or straw). Commercially available florist's staples of heavy-gauge galvanized aluminum are suited for heavier materials. (You can also make your own staples; see the directions on page 37.)

FLORIST'S PICKS

These 2½-inch (6.4cm) long pointed wooden sticks are wound with a length of fine-gauge wire for holding clusters of dried materials. Commercially available as wired green sticks, picks can also be made from a section of wooden skewer and some fine-gauge wire (see "Making Your Own Florist's Picks" on page 36).

ADHESIVE CLAY (FLORIST'S CLAY TAPE)

Adhesive clay or florist's clay tape is a band of clay that is available on a roll. Malleable and somewhat sticky, the clay is suited to adhering two lightweight materials. Adhesive clay can be molded into any shape and can be stored indefinitely.

NYLON STRING

Smooth, slippery, and soft, nylon string is kind to plant material. Use it for tying together bunches of foliage, wrapping stems, and hanging plant material.

SEWING THREAD

Sewing thread is useful in binding together delicate dried materials in small bunches that can later be inserted into the topiary head with a florist's pick. Available in all colors, sewing thread also comes in heavier weights such as quilting and carpet thread.

FLORIST'S CLAY

A malleable compound that feels like children's plastic clay, florist's clay is excellent for weighting containers. It is a less messy substitute for plaster.

ALL-PURPOSE WHITE GLUE

This glue is suited to bonding together lightweight, porous material such as single dried blooms and foliage. Dispensed in a creamy liquid from a plastic bottle, white glue applied in a thin layer requires from 5 to 10 minutes to dry completely, depending upon the density of the materials being bonded.

HOT GLUE GUN AND GLUE STICKS

Hot glue is essential for "instant" bonding of all materials, porous and nonporous. The electric gun dispenses a stream of heated glue that sets up in 4 to 10 seconds, depending on the materials being bonded. Choosing another bonding process or adhesive such as white glue, for example, would change the work time and possibly the end results.

Hot glue can cause burns; always use it cautiously, and keep a bowl of ice water nearby just in case. Never leave a hot glue gun unattended; keep it out of the reach of children.

FLORIST'S FOAM

Florist's foam is a commercially available plastic foam. The two types of florist's foam used in this book are referred to as Styrofoam or dry foam (Oasis).

Made from extruded plastic foam, Styrofoam has a rough texture; its surface dents easily. Stems to be inserted must be relatively strong since Styrofoam resists easy piercing by light- and medium-weight material. Styrofoam breaks into irregular chunks and melts easily under hot glue. Styrofoam is available in a variety of shapes (planks, bricks, spheres, and cones) and colors (green, brown, and white).

A finely granulated, denser plastic foam with a smooth texture, dry foam (Oasis) is available in bricks and spheres. Its color is usually dull green or brown. Most plant material pierces its surface easily, even the fragile stems of lavender. Dry foam can be sculpted into any shape. When making a large globe topiary, for example, you may not find a dry-foam sphere in the right size. To make your own, all you need are dry-foam blocks (two for a large sphere, one for a small sphere), packing tape (for a large sphere), and a serrated knife. To make a large sphere, tape two

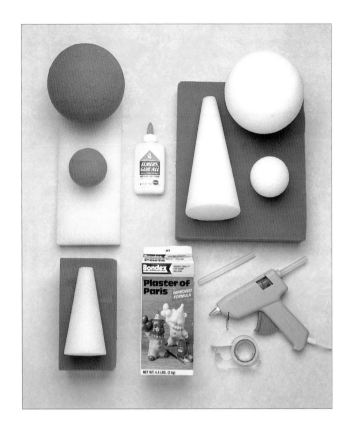

blocks of dry foam together with the packing tape, then use the knife to sculpt a sphere from the dry foam, slicing away the corners a sliver at a time.

Because it holds water for a very long time, dry foam can be used with fresh plant material. After it has been soaked, dry foam will take up to three weeks to dry fully, after which it can be reused.

PLASTER OF PARIS

A heavy white powder made of calcining gypsum, plaster of paris hardens to a dry, dense mass when mixed with water. It is useful for anchoring the stems of heavier topiaries and for weighting containers.

PACKING TAPE

Packing tape, which is reinforced with nylon threads, is excellent for securing heavy topiary heads to their stems or containers.

Chapter 2

TECHNIQUES FOR DRYING AND STORING PLANT MATERIAL

All the flowers and foliage featured in this book can be purchased from florists, craft stores, and growers. But you can also dry many floral varieties yourself and store them using the easy techniques described in this chapter. Drying your own plant material is economical. You can "recycle" cut flowers instead of throwing them away, or utilize favorite varieties from your own garden and seasonal varieties whose availability would otherwise be limited to their growing seasons.

Air-drying refers to the removal of moisture from plant material through evaporation. Plant material can be dried hanging upside down, standing upright, or lying flat. The method used is determined by the plant material: medium- and lightweight floral material can be hung upside down or stood upright depending on the variety; heavy, dense materials, as well as flat- and broad-leaved foliage, usually require a flat-drying method.

Dry chemical desiccants such as silica gel can also be used to remove the moisture from plant material. Desiccants are easy to use, are readily available, and produce good results.

AIR-DRYING

Dry all plant material in a dimly lit area, preferably a closet or attic where there is little humidity and no direct light. Because plant material will dry more slowly in a humid environment such as a kitchen or bathroom, it could wilt or form mold or rot. Direct sunlight will cause the colors to fade and make the petals and leaves brittle. Since fragile stems and flowers can break easily, plant material should not be moved too frequently while it is drying.

AIR-DRYING IN AN UPSIDE-DOWN POSITION (HANG-DRYING)

Hang-drying is the easiest and least expensive method for drying flowers and foliage. Fresh material is collected in a bunch, bound together with a rubber band, and hung upside down in a dry, dimly lit area. The speed of the evaporation of the water content in the flowers and foliage determines the drying time. Check the flower heads or leaves every day; when they feel like paper, they are dry enough for use as decoration.

Hang-Drying Roses

Roses dry very successfully, but you can apply this method to most other flowers and leaves. (If you do not have a suitable place to hang your fresh material, carefully insert the flower heads into a brown paper bag. Gather the bag around the stems and tie it with string to secure. Hang the bouquet upside down with string or wire.)

You Will Need:

16–20 fresh roses

Rubber bands

Nylon string (or medium-gauge
wire and wire cutters)

Clothesline or dowel suspended
between two points

1.

Lay the flowers on a worktable and strip away the leaves from the bottom ⅓ of each stem. (This will prevent mold and rot from developing on dense natural material.) Set the leaves aside.

AIR-DRYING IN AN UPRIGHT POSITION

Some flowers and foliage can be dried upright in a vase. In this method, plants such as hydrangea, eucalyptus, gypsophila, and acanthus gradually absorb water from a vase; the unabsorbed water is allowed to evaporate. Pampa grass and bulrush can be dried in an empty vase. Each stem will take on the contours of the original arrangement as it dries.

Drying Hydrangea in an Upright Position

You Will Need:

5-7 stems of mop-headed hydrangea

Vase

1.

Place the stems of the hydrangea in a vase with 1 inch (2.5cm) of water. Separate any flower heads that bump against one another so they won't flatten as they dry.

2.

When the water in the vase has evaporated and the flower heads feel like paper and are no longer pliable, the hydrangea are ready for use.

2.

Line up 8 to 10 stems, staggering the rose heads so they don't bump against one another.

3.

Lift the bunch by the stems, realigning any rose heads that are touching. Wrap a rubber band around the bottom of the stems to secure. (The rubber band will contract as the stems dry and reduce in diameter.)

4.

Invert the bunch and hang it up to dry (as shown above) using string or wire on a clothesline or dowel. Repeat the process for the remaining stems.

Note: For natural-looking curled leaves, gather 4 to 5 leaves by their stems and bind them together using sewing thread; hang them upside down until dry.

Drying Grasses and Pods in an Upright Position

Ornamental grasses, weeds, and pods can also be dried upright in a vase. The surfaces of some weeds should be sealed to prevent them from bursting into feathery wands.

You Will Need:

Bouquet of grasses, weeds, and pods

Newspaper

Pump hair spray

Vase

1.

Lay the fresh plant material on the newspaper and apply 3 light coats of hair spray.

2.

Arrange the plant material in a vase ⅛ full of water.

3.

Allow the water to evaporate.

AIR-DRYING IN A FLAT POSITION

Most foliage can be dried flat on a layer of newspaper or tissue placed in the bottom of a cardboard box or on an old window screen. Lightweight foliage often curls somewhat as it dries, but in most cases this natural curling is attractive. Some heavier plant materials, such as heavy leaves or large-petaled flowers, should be supported with wadded-up newspaper as they dry to maintain their natural shape.

Flat-drying is a good alternative when drying space is at a premium. The material can be laid in boxes, stacked, and stored until needed. Boxes should be long enough to allow the stems to fit without bending or breaking.

Drying Grasses, Twigs, Seed Heads, and Pods on Flat Newspaper

You Will Need:

Cardboard box

Newspaper

Selection of grasses (or chosen plant material)

1.

Line the bottom of a cardboard box with several sheets of newspaper.

2.

Lay the leaves on the bottom of the box in a row, allowing room around each stem for air circulation.

Drying Heavy Plant Material on Flat Chicken-Wire Screens

Heavier vegetation, foliage, and flowers can be dried individually on a framed screen made by stretching a length of chicken wire between two strips of wood and nailing it into place. The screen can be laid across two stacks of cinder blocks.

Chicken wire provides support for material while allowing air to circulate freely, preventing mold and rot from developing. Stems can also be inserted through the mesh for stability.

You Will Need:

Selection of heavy plant material, such as artichokes

Chicken wire frame or a length of chicken wire stretched across an open space and secured with heavy weights such as cinder blocks

1.

Insert the stem of each artichoke into one mesh of the chicken wire.

2.

Check the leaves of the artichokes every day or so. Artichokes may take up to 3 weeks to dry, depending upon humidity.

DRYING WITH DESICCANTS

The desiccants used for drying plant material are granular, moisture-absorbing agents such as silica gel and fine white sand. Both desiccants are effective and readily available.

When plant material is placed in a desiccant, the moisture in the plant is drawn into the desiccant crystals, leaving the material dry and ready for use as decoration. Two types of silica gel are available: one white, another with blue crystals that turn pink when they absorb moisture (and the plant material is dry).

There are several advantages to using desiccants for drying. Since desiccant crystals "embrace" the plant material entirely, the natural contour and color of the material is more accurately preserved. Desiccants have a high moisture-absorption rate that promotes the quick drying of plant material. In addition, both silica gel and sand can be reused: pour the used desiccant in a metal container, then place the container in a preheated (250°F [120°C]) oven to redry. The redried desiccant can be stored in an airtight container until it is needed.

Plastic containers with tightly sealed lids are most suitable for desiccant drying. Large, shallow food-storage containers can accommodate a generous amount of plant material without requiring too much desiccant. Flowers should be placed in the desiccant so they won't bump against one another. Because the number of blooms you can dry in a household container at one time is limited, you may want to set up several containers.

You need to take care with desiccants, though, as they can overdry your plant material. You should check the crystals every 2 days. If the colored crystals have turned pink or if the plant material is firm to the touch, gently brush away any desiccant and remove the specimen.

Because the plant material must fit a relatively shallow container, desiccant drying is usually used for flowers and foliage with short or nonexistent stems. (False stems can be added later by following the directions on page 31.) Flowers that have fragile petals (roses, peonies, camelias, and pansies) and leaves (rose leaves, oak, ferns, and ivy) are best suited to this method.

Drying Roses with Chemical Desiccants

You Will Need:

Plastic container with lid

1 pound (454g) of
silica gel crystals

Roses (or selection of
chosen plant material)

Soft artist's paintbrush

Teaspoon

Masking tape

1.

Fill the container to ½ inch (1.3cm) with silica gel crystals.

2.

Place the head of a rose faceup on the surface of the silica gel. Use the paintbrush to gently move the silica gel against the flower, filling all the spaces between the petals and leaves with crystals.

3.

Referring to the photograph, use the teaspoon to scoop up some silica gel and sprinkle it over the entire rose head. Repeat with the remaining roses.

4.

Place the lid on the container and seal it with masking tape. Store the container in a dry, dimly lit area.

5.

When the roses are dry, gently remove each flower head by its stem, pouring off the silica crystals as you lift it up. Use the paintbrush to clean off the petals.

DRYING WITH FINE WHITE SAND

Fine white sand does not have colored crystals to signal drying. But with a little care and vigilance, the sand can serve the purpose just as well. The method is the same as for silica gel, but the plant material must be checked every day so it doesn't overdry. Handle the plant material carefully; it becomes very fragile when dry.

STORING PLANT MATERIAL

Dried plant material may be stored for a year or so before using. The material must be packed carefully so it keeps its shape and color and does not rot. To prevent insect infestation, place a few mothballs in the storage box.

Storing Large-Headed Plant Material

Some large, heavy floral varieties such as mop-headed hydrangea, and vegetable varieties such as artichoke, should be wrapped separately when you store them.

You Will Need:

1 sheet of white tissue paper

Artichoke or hydrangea

One 6-inch (15.2cm) long medium-gauge stub wire

Cardboard box

1.

Crumple a sheet of tissue paper, then open it up. Place it on a flat worktable.

2.

Gather the paper along one side to form a cone.

3.

Hold the cone in your hand at the gathers and lay the stem of the plant material in the gather with the head pointing up.

4.

Wrap the plant material with the tissue, securing it at its stem with a wire.

5.

Store the plant material in a cardboard box.

Storing Dried Flowers

Flowers should be arranged loosely in a storage box to allow air circulation. Do not pack flowers on top of one another; moisture can collect and cause the material to develop mold or rot.

You Will Need:

Cardboard box

Newspaper

Dried flowers

Masking tape

1.

Line the bottom of the cardboard box with several sheets of newspaper. Place the dried flowers in a row on the bottom of the box.

2.

Place a length of masking tape across the stems just under their heads to hold the flowers in place.

3.

Lay a second row of dried stems just below the first row, allowing the heads of the second row to overlap the stems of the first row.

4.

Repeat Step 2 to secure the second row of dried floral material.

5.

Lightly cover the rows of dried material with several sheets of newspaper and cover the box. Store the box in a dry, dimly lit place.

Chapter 3

PREPARING PLANT MATERIAL

Most plant material needs some preparation before it can be used to decorate a topiary. Preparation techniques include four procedures: wiring and wrapping stems in order to reinforce weak or fragile stems, or to lengthen short stems; creating false stems for stemless flower heads and foliage; wiring single-headed stemless material, such as pinecones and pods; and wiring bunches of material together.

WIRING AND WRAPPING STEMS

By wiring and wrapping dried material you can create a strong stem that can stand independently or be inserted into the head of a topiary. The wire provides support for the original weaker stem; a wound layer of stem wrap secures the wire to the stem and conceals both.

A precut length of medium-gauge wire, also called stub wire, is usually used for reinforcing or lengthening stems. All types of stub wire—painted, unpainted, or cotton-wrapped—work well and can be used interchangeably for our purposes. Spool wire can also be used to wire a stem, but it must first be straightened. To do so, simply pull and stretch the desired length of wire with your hands.

When wiring flowers, choose a stub wire that is flexible, strong, and long enough to support the chosen stemmed material and a compatibly colored stem wrap. A false stem is usually attached to the stem, then trimmed to the final desired length when the topiary is being decorated. Therefore, you should choose a wire length that is the desired finished length of the stem (or a bit longer, if necessary). Fine-gauge wire is suited to fragile stems, while stronger, lower-gauge wire is suited to thicker stems.

WIRING FRAGILE-STEMMED FLOWERS

Many flowers, such as strawflowers, have thin stems that cannot support the weight of their own dried flower heads. Fine-gauge wire should be used to reinforce such delicate stems.

Wiring and Wrapping a Strawflower

You Will Need:

Rose wire

Teacup

One 6-inch (15.2cm) long fine-gauge stub wire

1 dried strawflower

Wire cutters

Stem wrap

Florist's scissors

1.

Place the spool of rose wire in a teacup and allow the wire to unreel. Place the stub wire against the stem, with the end of the wire gently resting on the underside of the flower head.

2.

Carefully draw the rose wire from its spool (without removing it from the teacup) and hold it against the stem/stub wire with the end of the rose wire pointing downward.

3.

Wind the rose wire around the stem/stub wire, overlapping all materials and trapping the loose end of rose wire.

4.

Bind the full length of the stem/stub wire; cut the end of the rose wire when finished.

5.

Hold the end of the stem wrap against the top section of the stem/stub wire with one hand, and the stem wrap with the other. Turn the stem/stub wire, wrapping the stem wrap at an angle around the full length of the stem. Cut the stem wrap and press the loose end to the end of the stem.

WIRING MEDIUM-STEMMED FLOWERS

Of all the medium-stemmed flowers used in topiary making, the dried rose is the most popular. The directions that follow can be applied to other medium-stemmed flowers or to any long- or short-stemmed flowers that need reinforcement or lengthening.

Wiring and Wrapping a Rose

You Will Need:

One 6-inch (15.2cm) long
medium-gauge stub wire

1 dried rose

Wire cutters

Green stem wrap

Florist's scissors

1.

Place the stub wire against the stem, with the end of the wire pushing gently on the underside of the rose head. Use the wire cutters to trim the stub wire, if necessary.

2.

Hold the end of the stem wrap against the top section of the stem/stub wire with one hand, and the stem wrap in the other.

3.

Pull on the stem wrap with one hand while turning the stem/stub wire with the other; angle the tape so it spirals down the entire length of the stem.

4.

Cut the stem wrap and squeeze the loose end against the stem to secure.

CREATING A FALSE STEM ON A FLOWER HEAD

Single-headed stemless flowers can be attached directly to a topiary with glue. But adding a false stem to a stemless flower head (or one with a very short stem) expands its possible design uses.

Wiring a False Stem on a Rose

Dried roses are beautiful but their heads often break off. You can easily create a false stem for rose heads using the method below.

You Will Need:

Pliers

One 6-inch (15.2cm) long
medium-gauge stub wire

1 dried rose

Wire cutters

Stem wrap

1.

Using the pliers, bend a small, narrow loop at one end of the stub wire, as shown in photograph A.

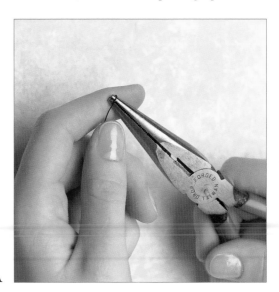

A

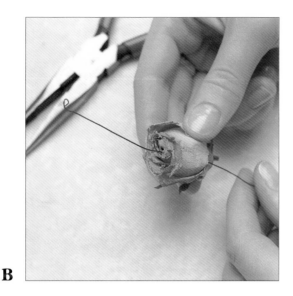

B

D

2.

Insert the other end of the wire down through the center of the rose head, exiting as close as possible to the center underside of the flower (see photograph B). Pull the wire down and draw the narrow loop into the flower head, parting any petals that might obstruct its path. Stop pulling when the loop is concealed in the flower head, as shown in photograph C, being careful not to pull the loop all the way through and out of the flower head. Wrap the wire around the stem two to three times to secure.

3.

Conceal the stub wire (photograph D) by wrapping the stem with stem wrap.

WIRING A FALSE STEM ON HARD, BRITTLE, OR SOFT MATERIAL

Natural dried materials that are stemless and particularly hard, brittle, or soft present special problems. Items in this category include pinecones, which resist piercing; poppyheads, which are very brittle; and fresh fruits and vegetables, which are soft and tear easily. These materials can add interesting texture and natural color to seasonal topiaries, but each requires a different method for adding a false stem.

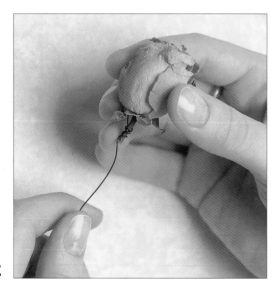

C

WIRING FRESH FRUITS AND VEGETABLES AND A POPPY POD

The method for creating a false stem on fresh fruits vegetables and poppy pods and is the same: the wire is inserted through the item itself. Lightweight pods, which are often brittle and require gentle handling, can be wired with fine-gauge wire and displayed in almost any position. Stems for heavier fruits and vegetables should be made from heavier-gauge wire. These items must be displayed with some type of support so that the wired stem does not rip out under its own weight. This can be done by positioning them so that the Styrofoam helps support their weight. You can also insert a toothpick or a section cut from a wooden skewer underneath any of these heavier decorations to provide additional support.

Wiring Fruits and Vegetables

You Will Need:

1 piece of fruit or vegetable
(lady apple, brussels sprouts, or
lemons work well)

One 8-inch (20.3cm) long
medium-gauge stub wire

1.

Holding the fruit or vegetable in one hand and the stub wire in the other, pierce the skin of the fruit or vegetable at its lower ⅓ with the wire. Push the wire through and out the other side.

2.

Bend the two free ends of the wire down and under the item, twisting them together to secure.

Wiring a Pod

You Will Need:

Rose wire

Teacup

Wire cutters

Sewing needle

1 stemless poppyhead

White or brown stem wrap

1 florist's pick (optional)

1.

Place the spool of rose wire in the teacup and allow the wire to unreel. Draw the wire from the spool (without removing it from the teacup) and use the wire cutters to cut a 6-inch (15.2cm) length.

2.

Use the sewing needle to poke a tiny hole on opposite sides of the lower portion of the pod.

3.

Insert one end of the wire into one hole, gently guiding the wire across and through the other hole until 3 inches (7.6cm) of the wire protrudes.

4.

Gently bend the wire ends beneath the pod head, twisting them to secure.

5.

Conceal the wire ends with stem wrap. If necessary, attach the false stem to a florist's pick if the item is to be inserted in resistant material.

Wiring a Pinecone

The pinecone is sturdy and easy to handle. Its collar of scales makes a good anchor for a false stem.

You Will Need:

1 pinecone

One 6-inch (15.2cm) long
medium-gauge stub wire

Pliers

Wire cutters

General-purpose scissors

Brown stem wrap

1.

Holding the pinecone in your hand, center the stub wire against the back of the bottom row of scales (see photograph A). Bend the free lengths of wire around to the front, fitting the lengths of wire carefully between the scales.

A

B

2.

Twist the ends of the wire tightly in front, making certain that the pinecone does not twist freely within the wire collar.

3.

Use the pliers to bend the ends of the wire down and press them against the underside of the base of the pinecone (see photograph B). Use the wire cutters to trim the stub wire, if necessary.

4.

Conceal the wire with stem wrap.

WIRING BUNCHES

Wiring several stems of plant material together has several advantages. It allows you to attach a bunch of flowers or foliage to the base material at once and achieve broad, quick coverage of the topiary. Also, because a bunch of stems is added with a single stub wire or florist's pick, the base material is less likely to weaken and crumble over time.

Wiring bunches means exactly that: gathering stems of plant material, wiring them into a small bouquet, and using the wire as a false stem. The bunch can also be wired to a florist's pick.

Wiring a Bunch with Stub Wire

Because the technique for wiring bunches with stub wire is the same for most thin and medium-thick stems of plant material, the following directions can be used to prepare the stems of a single variety (such as statice or baby's breath), or a mixed variety (such as roses, statice, and cockscomb). Stub wire allows you to gather a large number of stems (up to 1½-inch [3.8cm] diameter) in one bouquet.

You Will Need:

1 bunch of dried flowers
(4-6 stems with a ¾-inch
[1.9cm] diameter)

Florist's scissors

Stem wrap

One 8-inch (20.3cm) long
medium-gauge stub wire

Wire cutters (optional)

1.

Align the heads of all flowers on a flat work surface. Using the florist's scissors, trim all the stems even to 2½ inches (6.4cm) to create a small bouquet.

2.

Hold the bouquet by the stems and wrap the stems with stem wrap (see photograph A). Place the stub wire against the stems, leaving 1 inch (2.5cm) extend-

B

ing below the trimmed ends and the opposite end of the wire extending into the flowers or foliage (see photograph B).

3.

Referring to photograph C, bend the top wire down and wind it around the stub wire and stems for the full length of the stems.

4.

Twist together the ends of the wire extending below the stem ends.

5.

Use the wire cutters to trim the stub wire neatly, if necessary.

A

C

Wiring a Bunch with a Florist's Pick

A florist's pick—a length of fine-gauge wire attached to a slender wooden pick—can also be used to affix a small bouquet of dried material to a topiary head. Because the picks are relatively long and thick, take care not to insert too many in a small area, as this could cause the foam base to crumble.

You Will Need:

6 slender stems
of dried material

Florist's scissors

Stem wrap

1 florist's pick

1.

Lay the dried material on a flat work surface and trim the stems even using florist's scissors.

2.

Hold the dried heads of the floral material in one hand and wrap the stems with stem wrap (see photograph A on page 35). Carefully wind the wire attached to the florist's pick around the bound stems just under the floral heads. Twist the wire ends to secure.

3.

Position and insert the florist's pick into the foam base material.

Making Your Own Florist's Picks

If florist's picks are not available, you can easily make your own by using lengths of wooden skewer and fine-gauge wire.

You Will Need:

General-purpose scissors

1 wooden skewer

One 4-inch (10.2cm) long
fine-gauge wire

1.

Use the scissors to cut a 2½-inch (6.4cm) length of skewer from one pointed end.

2.

Center and wrap the wire around the blunt end of the cut skewer.

3.

Use the pick to bind and attach the chosen floral material as described in the directions given in the previous column.

Wiring a Bunch with a Florist's Staple

Florist's staples—purchased or those you make your-self—can be used to attach several stems of dried material onto a topiary head.

You Will Need:

4–6 slender (or 3 thick) stems of
dried material

Florist's scissors

Stem wrap

1 commercially made
florist's staple

1.

Lay the stems of the dried material on a flat work surface and trim them to 2½ inches (6.4cm) with the florist's scissors.

2.

Bind the stems together with stem wrap.

3.

To decorate a topiary using bunches of dried flowers and florist's staples, position the bunch on the surface of the foam, then straddle the florist's staple across the stems near the flower heads. Push the wire legs into the foam until only the staple crossbar shows. Conceal the staple crossbar with the heads of the next bunch of dried material.

Making Your Own Florist's Staples

Because purchased florist's staples are relatively large, they could crumble the foam base of a small topiary. For small projects that use fragile-stemmed flowers you can make florist's staples of any size from medium-gauge wire.

You Will Need:

Wire cutters

One 6-inch (15.2cm) long
medium-gauge stub wire or
one 6-inch (15.2cm) long
medium-gauge spool wire

Pliers

1.

Use the wire cutters to cut the stub wire into two 3-inch (7.6cm) lengths; or unroll and cut two 3-inch (7.6cm) lengths of medium-gauge spool wire.

2.

Bend one length of wire into a horseshoe shape using pliers; repeat with the second wire length.

3.

Use the staples to attach chosen floral material to a topiary head as described in the directions given in the previous column.

Chapter 4

CONSTRUCTION METHODS AND DESIGN PRINCIPLES

There are three basic methods of constructing a topiary: the dome, the globe, and the standard. These methods are the foundations for all the topiary variations featured in this book.

The components of the topiary include the head, the container, and, in some cases, the stem. By manipulating certain variables—the size of each component, proportion among components, and the choice of decorative materials—you can create different effects. The color and texture of the decorative material, the kinds of plant material you choose, and the manner in which you place it on the topiary are all important elements of communicating a particular style or feeling, or suggesting a season or holiday.

This chapter will offer guidance in understanding the principles of good topiary design. Once you have mastered the basic construction techniques, you can go on to create your own designs using any materials or combinations you wish.

THE DOME TOPIARY

The dome topiary comprises two basic components: the head and the container. The head, often made from dry foam (Oasis), is usually shaped like a mound. It rises up from the opening of the container and is decorated with plant material. The proportion of the topiary head to container is very much a question of personal taste, but the container must be heavy enough to support the decorated head.

THE GLOBE TOPIARY

Similar to the dome topiary, the globe topiary contains an additional component—a trunk or stem. The trunk is usually a straight column representing the trunk of a tree; it connects the head of the topiary with the container. The proportion among the three components is usually ½ head, ¼ trunk, and ¼ container. However, there is no hard and fast rule for determining the size of each component. The head of the topiary is the focal point and usually of some weight; the trunk must visually support the size of the decorated head, balance it visually with the container, and anchor any top weight.

To prevent a topiary from tipping over, you can weight any container with florist's clay, or you can use an inexpensive terra-cotta pot filled with plaster of paris as the primary container, which can later be placed into a decorative container (see page 42).

DECORATING THE DOME AND GLOBE TOPIARY

After it is constructed, a dome or globe topiary requires some type of decorative covering. Decorating a topiary can be as simple as applying sheet moss to the entire surface of the head, or as relatively complex as attaching bouquets of flowers and foliage in a particular pattern. Again, personal taste rules: when you have mastered the basic construction techniques, you can substitute one color flower or type of leaf for another and choose the decorative materials that are most appealing to you.

THE STANDARD TOPIARY

The standard may appear to be the simplest topiary to make. But a well-designed standard topiary depends on the manipulation and balance of a complex set of variables.

The standard is the only topiary that is constructed and decorated in the same procedure. Completely different in construction from the other two topiary types, the standard requires that the plant material stand up straight, either in a loose bouquet bound with string, raffia, or ribbon, or in small bunches in a flat-bottomed container. The foam in the container is usually concealed with moss that has been hot-glued, put in place with florist's staples, or tucked into the sides of the container. Designs for the standard topiary vary from a simple bouquet of wheat to more studied combinations of plant material, such as a patchwork pattern of flower heads. In the single bouquet using one kind of material, the contour and texture become the focus; in the studied design approach, it is the pattern of neat rows and sections that draw the focus.

Design possibilities are limited only by the character of the dried materials and the container into which they are placed. The color, type, and texture of the plant materials as well as the height, width, and pattern they create when placed in the base all affect the appearance of the standard topiary—and almost any combination works technically.

BASIC CONSTRUCTION TECHNIQUES

In the pages that follow: you will find instructions for creating the topiary styles featured in this book.

Constructing the Basic Dome Topiary

The dome topiary has two components: the head and the container. A lightweight dome topiary does not require a weighted container. But if the planned decoration makes the topiary top-heavy, you can place florist's clay in the bottom of the container to counterbalance the weight of the head.

You Will Need:

Container with a round opening

Adhesive clay
(florist's clay tape)*

1 dry-foam sphere with a
diameter slightly larger than the
opening of the container

*Option: substitute low-melt glue
gun and glue sticks, if desired.

A

1.

Place the container on a flat work surface.

2.

Press a length of adhesive clay onto the full circumference of the inner top rim of the pot (see photograph A). (You could also use the low-melt glue gun to apply a stream of glue on the inner top rim.)

3.

Push the sphere into the container so that the clay (or glue) forms a tight bond between the sphere and the inner edge of the container's opening (see photograph B).

B

Constructing the Basic Globe Topiary

The basic components of the globe topiary are the head, the stem, and the container. If the head is heavy when decorated, or rises up too high over the container, shifting the center of gravity, the container must be weighted (see the directions that follow in the next column).

You Will Need:

Serrated knife

Dry-foam block, 9 inches (22.9cm) long × 4 inches (10.2cm) wide × 3 inches (7.6cm) high

Terra-cotta pot, 3½ inches (8.9cm) in diameter, 3 inches (7.6cm) high

Dry-foam sphere, 3 inches (7.6cm) in diameter

8-inch (20.3cm) long dowel, ¼ inch (0.6cm) in diameter

Adhesive clay (florist's clay tape)

1.

Use the serrated knife to sculpt the foam block to fit the container snugly. Insert the foam into the container and trim it even with the rim of the pot.

2.

Center and impale the foam sphere on the dowel, but do not allow the dowel to poke through the top of the sphere. Apply a narrow collar of adhesive clay around the dowel to secure the sphere.

3.

Making sure that the dowel is perpendicular to the pot, center and insert the other end of the dowel into the foam in the container.

Constructing the Basic Globe Topiary with a Weighted Container

In this method, plaster of paris is used to weight the container to counterbalance the topiary's heavy head and stabilize the construction. Never pour plaster directly into a fine pot made of china. Plaster expands as it hardens and will cause the china to crack. Instead, follow the directions below and place the weighted terra-cotta pot into the more valuable container afterward.

You Will Need:

Saber saw

Dowel

Dry-foam wedges

Terra-cotta pot

Adhesive clay (florist's clay tape)

Plaster of paris

Plastic mixing container

Wooden paint stirrer

Dry-foam sphere

Packing tape, ¾ inch (1.9cm) wide

1.

Following a ratio of head to stem to container of 2:1:1, use the saber saw to cut the dowel the length of the overall height of the topiary; set it aside.

2.

Place wedges of dry foam on the bottom of the container, then place foam wedges at even intervals all around the interior of the container (see photograph A; the number of wedges necessary is in direct proportion to the size of your container.) The dry-foam wedges will act as a cushion to prevent the container

A

B

6.

from cracking as the plaster of paris hardens. If necessary, you can use a bit of adhesive clay to secure the foam.

3.

Prepare the plaster of paris following the package directions. Fill the container with the wet plaster, to about ½ inch (1.3cm) below the rim.

4.

Insert the cut dowel into the center of the wet plaster, making certain that the dowel is straight when viewed from all angles (see photograph B).

5.

Hold the dowel in place until it is secure (this will take about 3 to 4 minutes). The plaster will continue to harden for an hour or so. Let the plaster harden completely before proceeding to step 6.

Impale the dry-foam sphere on the dowel, pushing with even pressure in a vertical direction until the top of the sphere just meets the top of the dowel. (Do not wiggle the sphere as you push down; it will make the channel too wide and cause the head to wobble on its trunk.) Add a narrow collar of adhesive clay to secure the sphere to the dowel. (When making globe topiaries of substantial weight, cut a length of packing tape in half lengthwise, then crisscross the two tape lengths over the top of the sphere. Wrap the loose ends around the dowel just beneath the sphere to secure it.)

7.

Insert or glue dried flowers to decorate the head of the stem. Conceal the plaster with moss or other suitable plant material.

Constructing the Basic Standard Topiary

In this method, upright stems of plant material are inserted one at a time into a foam base.

You Will Need:

Dried plant material
(14 rose stems and a 4-inch
[10.2cm] square of sheet moss)

Florist's scissors

1 dry-foam sphere with a
diameter slightly larger than the
opening of the container

Container with a 4-inch
(10.2cm) round opening

Serrated knife or saber saw

Florist's staples

$\frac{1}{2}$ yard (45.7cm) of
ribbon or raffia

1.

Lay the stems of the plant material on a flat work surface, heads even. Use florist's scissors to trim the bottom of the stems even.

2.

Push the sphere into the pot. With the knife or saber saw, slice away the extra foam, making sure that the remaining foam is even with the rim of the pot (see photograph A).

3.

One by one, insert the stems of the plant material, making sure that the flower heads are even (see photograph B).

4.

Conceal the foam by stapling sheet moss, torn to size, to its surface. Gently tie the ribbon or raffia around the flower stems to secure the arrangement (see photograph C).

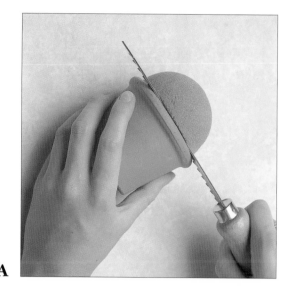

A

B

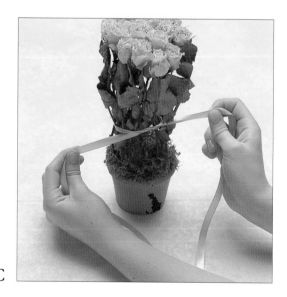

C

Constructing the Patchwork Standard Topiary

The patchwork standard topiary utilizes the same techniques used to create a basic standard. But in this case, several kinds of plant material, chosen primarily for their color, are inserted into a base of foam in a preconceived pattern. The design is often called patchwork because it resembles the geometry of pieced quilts. For the purpose of illustration, four types of material were used.

You Will Need:

Serrated knife

1 to 2 blocks of dry foam (equal to the area of the container)

Flat-bottomed container

Spool wire

Florist's scissors

Dried plant material in 4 different colors

1.

Use the serrated knife to trim the dry foam so that it fits snugly into the container. Trim the foam even with the top rim.

2.

Mark 4 triangular sections in the foam: stretch a length of spool wire diagonally over the foam and press the wire into the foam to create an indentation. Repeat on the other diagonal.

3.

Use the florist's scissors to cut the stems of all plant material: for a low standard, cut all stems to the height of the container plus 1½ inches (3.8cm); for a high standard, cut the stems 6 to 10 inches (15.2 to 25.4cm) above the rim of the container.

4.

Insert the stems of one color of plant material perpendicular to the foam, densely filling one triangular section.

5.

Insert the second color plant material into the opposite triangular section, followed by the third and fourth colors. The entire top of the foam should be filled with plant material.

CREATING VARIATIONS ON THE PATCHWORK STANDARD TOPIARY

The technical principle of standing up dried material in marked patterns is the underpinning of all possible variations on the standard topiary. However, each variation usually highlights one feature—for instance, the different heights of material in a tiered standard, the contrast between bands of single-color varieties, or the textured effect created by mixing varieties of same-color dried materials.

To create the variations described here, refer to the materials list in "Constructing the Patchwork Standard Topiary" on this page. Then follow the directions on this page and the next for preparing and inserting the dried flowers.

THE TIERED STANDARD

Raise the stems of one color of plant material in marked sections opposite one another. Or create tiers by inserting the dried material in descending heights working toward the front of the container.

The Monochromatic Standard

Use 4 shades of one color to create subtle contrast in color among marked sections.

The Contrasting Color Standard

Use 4 contrasting colors, such as orange and purple, light green and burgundy, to create bold sections of contrasting color.

The Bouquet Standard

The bouquet standard is the purest example of the standard topiaries. Dried material is simply gathered in a bouquet with the stems in a vertical position. It is displayed upright or upside down.

You Will Need:

6 to 10 bunches of long-stemmed plant material

Florist's scissors

Nylon string

Ribbon or raffia

1.

Lay the stems of the plant material on a flat work surface, heads even. Use florist's scissors to trim the bottom of the stems even.

2.

Gather the stems and hold them upright; tap the bottom edge of the stems gently on the work surface to even them.

3.

Tie the string around the middle of the plant material to secure it.

4.

Conceal the string with a ribbon bow or a rope-width thickness of raffia.

Design Principles

The attraction of topiary making is that it is not only easy—it is easy to achieve a pleasing design. When an overall design is appealing, it is usually the result of balancing several variables: the overall size and shape of the topiary, and the colors and textures of the basic components.

Size and Shape

Topiaries can range in height from 5 inches (12.7cm) to over 3 feet (91.4cm), and from an overall width of just 3½ inches (8.9cm) to over 1½ feet (45.7cm). In general, the height and width are planned in proportion to one another so that the topiary is physically and visually balanced. If you look at the topiaries in this book as if they were silhouettes, you will begin to understand this relationship and be able to design your own topiaries accordingly.

The dome topiary, with its head seated on a container, is designed to present solidity. The globe topiary is slightly more refined and generally more poetic in feel. The stem that separates the base container from the topiary head allows the eye to move more freely, resulting in a lighter, less compact effect. The standard topiary is a hybrid of sorts in that the dried material itself can create a subtle or strong impact, depending on the combinations used and the patterns those combinations form. Standard topiaries can be majestic—for instance, tall stalks of dried material standing in straight rows—or whimsical—crisscrossed bands of dried material in a shallow box.

Size and shape must serve to balance the topiary physically. But size and shape also combine in an overall visual configuration that communicates style and attitude—and it is in this aspect that you have immense creative freedom. Choose the overall silhouette you prefer and manipulate the proportions according to the setting in which it will be placed.

Consider using a square container in combination with a conical head; use a cylindrical container and a cylindrical head; or stack several spheres on a central stem and anchor them to an urn-shaped container. There are no rules for manipulating the geometry of the basic components. Plan your own design: sketch it on a piece of paper first, changing the components until you are satisfied. Then gather your materials and let the fun begin.

COLOR AND TEXTURE

Your choice of dried material will also convey the message of design and style. Whether purchased or home grown, flowers and foliage are available in an endless variety of colors and textures. It is sometimes difficult to know which combinations will work well together. Before beginning a project, it is a good idea to collect many samples of dried material and place them together in different combinations. This way you can be more sure of being satisfied with the color and textural relationships.

Of course, your decorating style will influence your choices, too. If your home has a traditional English interior, you may gravitate toward soft shades of rose and blue, selecting roses and strawflowers to further carry the theme. In a Southwest-style interior, you may choose peaches and sea foam greens, painted pods, and broad-leaved foliage. You might even wish to borrow the palette from an upholstery or drapery swatch so that your topiary design coordinates with your living space.

Consider your dried materials as an artist might regard paint. The principles of coordinating colors to achieve a design with impact relate clearly to the principles of the color wheel. When the primary colors—red, blue, and yellow—are used in combination or alone, they make a strong statement. (Imagine an arrangement of red roses, blue larkspur, and golden yarrow.) Primary colors suggest the warmer months, when reds, blues, and yellows abound in nature.

When the primary colors are mixed a second level of colors results. These secondary colors—orange, purple, and green—also create a strong look. You'll find them in a wide range of hues in nature such as purple statice, orange safflower, and green leaves of every description. If you approach dried floral varieties with these basic understandings you will be able to plan designs that please you. For inspiration, you might want to keep a file of illustrations taken from magazines, botanical drawings, postcards of favorite paintings, and the like. There are also many books on color harmony and theory; check your local library, bookstore, or art supply store.

Texture, intrinsic to dried floral material, is a design element that carries great impact when used in arrangements where the plant material is of one color or color family. Presented in feathery grasses and pods, sensuously curved stems, or staccato dots of miniature daisies, texture adds visual interest without introducing a new color. To emphasize texture, combine dramatically different materials—velvety cockscomb and spiky strawflowers, for example. As you become familiar with the variety of dried material available, you can use texture to amplify the drama of your designs.

Part Two

THE
TOPIARY
COLLECTION

Chapter 5

THE DOME TOPIARY

MINIATURE ROSEBUDS IN A TERRA-COTTA POT

The rosebud topiary is perhaps one of the most popular dried-flower arrangements, and it is also very easy to make: rows of miniature rosebuds are simply hot-glued to a dome of dry foam.

This design is as practical as it is beautiful, as any flower heads can be used as decoration. Miniature strawflowers and globe amaranth are attractive alternatives to the roses, and because the heads of these flowers are somewhat larger, you will need less material to cover the dome.

A simple terra-cotta pot was chosen as the container for this arrangement because of its straightforward shape and subtle color, but other small containers would work just as well. A china teacup or a small bandbox covered in a small-print wallpaper, for example, would be a pretty substitute.

Finished Size: 4½ inches (11.4cm) high, 4 inches (10.2cm) wide

You Will Need:

Terra-cotta pot, 3 inches (7.6cm) high, with a 3¼-inch (8.3cm) diameter opening

Adhesive clay (florist's clay tape)

Dry-foam sphere, 4 inches (10.2cm) in diameter

Hot glue gun and glue sticks

75 pink miniature rosebuds

1.

Place the terra-cotta pot on a flat work surface.

2.

Press a length of adhesive clay onto the inner top rim of the pot, creating a clay collar around the entire circumference.

3.

Push the sphere into the opening of the pot, squeezing the clay between the foam sphere and the inner edge of the pot opening to create a tight seal.

4.

To decorate the dome, hot-glue rosebuds around the lower perimeter of the foam in a tight ring with the buds touching the pot rim and radiating outward.

5.

Continue hot-gluing buds in even rings, working from bottom to top, until the dry foam is concealed.

GOLD NUTS AND PODS IN A TERRA-COTTA POT

Small dome topiaries can be put together quickly, which makes them ideal gifts. You can combine a wide variety of small items, including dried and silk flowers with small heads, foliage, nuts, pods, beads, and even Christmas tree ornaments.

For the holidays, pinecones and holly make a fanciful arrangement, as shown here. Simply choose your material, arrange it on the dome, and secure it either with hot glue or by inserting it directly into the foam, then accent the arrangement with a ribbon.

Finished Size: 5 inches (12.7cm) high, 5½ inches (14cm) wide

You Will Need:

Terra-cotta pot, 3 inches (7.6cm) high, with a 4-inch (10.2cm) diameter opening

Adhesive clay (florist's clay tape)

Dry-foam sphere, 4½ inches (11.4cm) in diameter

1 pinecone

3 miniature lotus pods

3 poppyheads

4 nutmeg nuts

6 small holly leaves

4 heads of silk Queen Anne's lace

Newspaper

Gold spray paint

Wire cutters or general-purpose scissors

Hot glue gun and glue sticks

½ yard (45.7cm) of green wire-edged ribbon with gold borders, 1 inch (2.5cm) wide

1.

Prepare the pot following Steps 1–3 of Miniature Rosebuds in a Terra-Cotta Pot on page 50.

2.

Lay the decorative material on the newspaper and spray paint it gold, following the manufacturer's directions. (Be sure to work in a well-ventilated room.) Let the material dry.

3.

Use the wire cutters or scissors to trim the silk floral stems to 2 inches (5.1cm).

4.

Hot-glue the gold decorative elements, one at a time, in a pleasing arrangement on top of the dome of dry foam (refer to the photograph as a guide for placement).

5.

Tie the ribbon in a bow around the pot.

GOLD AND RUST FLOWERS IN A CHINA POT

Instead of using only one type of flower, this topiary combines a variety of flowers and foliage of one colorway. The appeal of this topiary is that the head has a subtle box shape, made possible by using an uncut block of dry foam in the container instead of the traditional sphere.

Using one colorway is an effective way to communicate the feeling of a particular season. For spring, pastel blooms make for a very pretty combination, while red roses, burgundy and green-dyed cockscomb, and holly leaves sprayed gold are nice for the winter or Christmas. Tying a cord and tassel around the outside of a decorative pot or wrapping pretty gift wrap around a simple terra-cotta planter makes the arrangement a perfect gift.

Finished Size: 14 inches (35.6cm) high, 12 inches (30.5cm) wide

You Will Need:

Dry-foam block, 9 inches (22.9cm) long × 4 inches (10.2cm) wide × 3 inches (7.6cm) high

Painted and glazed china pot, 5½ inches (14cm) high with a 5-inch (12.7cm) diameter opening

Adhesive clay (florist's clay tape)

Packing tape

Florist's scissors

30 rust safflower blossoms and buds

20 yellow strawflowers

12 orange strawflowers

16 sunflowers

12 yellow tea roses

1.

Center and attach the dry-foam block over the pot opening: press small strips of adhesive clay over contact points and crisscross strips of packing tape over the top center of the dry foam, attaching the loose ends to the sides of the pot to secure.

2.

Use the florist's scissors to trim the stems of all dried flowers to 4½ inches (11.4cm).

3.

Insert the safflower stems evenly around the foam, making sure they radiate outward.

4.

Continue inserting flowers, one variety at a time, all around the block, distributing them evenly.

5.

Cover the entire block with dried material, filling in any bare spots with extra flowers.

MIXED FLOWERS
IN AN URN

Perhaps the easiest of all topiaries to make, this particular arrangement is made by placing a large foam sphere in the opening of a low urn, then decorating it. This arrangement can be densely and lushly decorated, as its heavy container and attendant low center of gravity make it very stable. Because of this, you can insert dried material with long stems to create a sweeping, overgrown look. This topiary is large enough to place in an entrance foyer, or next to a fireplace during the warmer months.

Finished Size: 18 inches (45.7cm) high, 16 inches (40.6cm) wide

You Will Need:

Iron urn painted white, 8 inches (20.3cm) high, with a 10-inch (25.4cm) diameter opening

Newspaper

Dry-foam sphere, 12 inches (30.5cm) in diameter

Packing tape

Florist's scissors

20 branches of melaleuca foliage

8–10 stems of yellow tansy

10 stems of yellow craspedia

40 stems of red phalaris

20 branches of oregano

1.

Fill the bottom cavity of the urn with crumpled newspaper; then place the dry-foam sphere on top, crisscrossing the packing tape over the top center of the foam and attaching the tape ends to the sides of the urn to secure.

2.

Use the florist's scissors to cut the stems of the foliage, tansy, craspedia, and phalaris to 5 inches (12.7cm); cut the stems of the oregano to 3 inches (7.6cm).

3.

Insert the stems of the oregano into the foam, making sure they radiate outward and are distributed evenly around the dome.

4.

Continue inserting floral material, one variety at a time, distributing it evenly and fully. Alternate the heights of adjacent flowers for an airy effect by pushing some stems deeper into the foam than others.

5.

Finish by inserting the stems of melaleuca foliage.

Boxwood in an Urn

Simple, classic, and elegant, this dome topiary is a favorite. Made from only one type of foliage, boxwood painted hunter green, the decorated head of this topiary rests in the opening of a majestic urn. Here, too, the urn serves to anchor the large head of the topiary, while its rich, boot-black color adds a nice contrast to the shiny green leaves. A rope and tassel can be added for a dramatic touch.

Painted boxwood, however, tends to be expensive, particularly if purchased from a florist or craft store. Fortunately, one stem of boxwood goes far because it is very branchy, that is, many short sections can be snipped from one stem.

If you have a boxwood bush, you can bleach the stems yourself for a different look. To do this, you need to construct the topiary first, using the freshly cut stems of fresh boxwood to decorate the head of the topiary (if you bleached out the boxwood first, the stems would become fragile and the leaves would drop off). When the topiary is finished, it should be moved in front of a sunny window and turned often to insure that it bleaches evenly. A full bleaching should occur in 2 to 3 weeks, depending on the season and the intensity of the sun's rays.

Finished Size: 34 inches (86.4cm) high, 24 inches (61cm) wide

You Will Need:

Adhesive clay (florist's clay tape)

Urn, 21 inches (53.3cm) high, with a 10-inch (25.4cm) diameter opening

Premolded foam sphere, 12 inches (30.5cm) in diameter

Packing tape

Pruning shears

160 branches of boxwood, painted or dyed dark green

Rope and tassel (optional)

1.

Press adhesive clay onto the inner rim of the urn, then press the sphere firmly onto the rim, creating a secure seal.

2.

Crisscross 2 lengths of packing tape over the top center of the sphere and attach the ends to the sides of the urn.

3.

Use the pruning shears to trim the boxwood branches into 5-inch (12.7cm) stems. Beginning at the top center of the sphere, insert the boxwood in the foam, placing the stems close together with the foliage radiating outward.

4.

Continue inserting the boxwood stems in the foam until the sphere is covered.

5.

If desired, loosely tie a rope and tassel around the urn as shown.

ROSES AND MOSS ON A CANDLESTICK

Candlesticks made from virtually any material, such as glass or metal, offer elegant contrast to the rounded colorful contour of a topiary head by providing a slender base for the arrangement. In this particular case, the sophisticated lines and traditional shape of a brass candlestick inspired the choice of the dried plant material. Romantic pale pink roses were selected because their color complements the brass; also, the stems are strong and easily pierce the dry-foam sphere. The moss was chosen for its subtle green color and for the ease with which it can fill in the rows between the roses.

Finished Size: 14 inches (35.6cm) high

You Will Need:

10 lemon leaves or salal

Newspaper

Gold spray paint

Adhesive clay (florist's clay tape)

Candlestick, 4 inches (10.2cm) high

Premolded foam sphere, 6 inches (15.2cm) in diameter

Packing tape

Hot glue gun and glue sticks

Florist's scissors

72 pink tea roses

12 ounces (336g) of reindeer moss

1.

Lay the leaves on newspaper and spray paint them gold, following the manufacturer's directions. Let them dry.

2.

Press pieces of adhesive clay onto the rim of the candle cup, then press the foam sphere onto the clay. Secure the sphere by crisscrossing 2 lengths of packing tape on the top center of the sphere; attach the loose ends around the neck of the candle cup.

3.

Hot-glue the gold leaves around the bottom of the sphere in a radiating pattern.

4.

Using the scissors, trim the stems of the roses to 3½ inches (8.9cm); insert them in rings around the sphere as shown.

5.

Hot-glue bunches of moss in the remaining spaces between the rows of roses.

Chapter 6

THE GLOBE TOPIARY

TEA ROSES ON A GOLDEN STEM

Sweet and romantic, this globe topiary combines three basic elements: a head of tea roses, a stem made from a painted gold dowel, and a whitewashed terra-cotta container. The simplicity of its construction makes this arrangement an especially appealing first globe topiary. Virtually any flower heads can be substituted for the roses.

This globe topiary can be made in a larger scale; just keep the proportions the same. Make certain, though, that the dried material does not become top-heavy, as this will cause the topiary to topple over. Weighting the bottom of the pot with florist's clay will help prevent this from happening.

Finished Size: 10½ inches (26.7cm) high, 5½ inches (14cm) wide

You Will Need:

10-inch (25.4cm) long dowel or stick, ¼ inch (0.6cm) in diameter

Newspaper

Gold spray paint

Serrated knife

2 dry-foam spheres, each 3 inches (7.6cm) in diameter

Whitewashed terra-cotta container, 2 inches (5.1cm) high, with a 3-inch (7.6cm) diameter opening

Adhesive clay (florist's clay tape)

Florist's scissors

48–72 tea rose heads

3-inch (7.6cm) disk of sheet moss

1.

Lay the dowel on a sheet of newspaper. Following the manufacturer's directions, spray paint the dowel gold; let it dry.

2.

Use the serrated knife to sculpt one foam sphere to fit the container snugly.

3.

Insert the dowel into the second sphere. Press a narrow collar of adhesive clay underneath the sphere to secure.

4.

Insert the opposite end of the dowel into foam in the container.

5.

Use the florist's scissors to trim the stems of the tea roses to 1 inch (2.5cm); then insert the stems, one at a time, into the foam sphere to cover it completely.

6.

Conceal the foam in the container with the sheet moss.

SHEET MOSS IN AN ANTIQUED POT

Sheet moss, with its rich texture and mottled green color, makes a wonderful decorative cover for the head of a topiary or base of a container. As shown here, sheet moss doesn't need to be accented with flowers or other decoration; it can easily stand alone.

Moss comes live in the form of folded sheets with some of the soil still attached. When making a large topiary, the soil does not affect the application process. But with a small topiary like this, it is necessary to shake off some of the soil so that the remaining sheet is thin enough to adhere to the contours of the small sphere without bunching up or adding weight to the topiary head.

A variation on the previous topiary, this design requires only sheet moss for decoration and an easy sponging technique to lend the terra-cotta pot a weathered look.

Finished Size: 8½ inches (21.6cm) high, 3½ inches (8.9cm) wide

You Will Need:

White acrylic paint

Waxed paper

Household sponge

Terra-cotta pot, 3 inches (7.6cm) high, with a 3-inch (7.6cm) diameter opening

Serrated knife

2 dry-foam spheres, each 3 inches (7.6cm) in diameter

8-inch (20.3cm) long natural stick or dowel, ¼ inch (0.6cm) in diameter

Adhesive clay (florist's clay tape)

Small paintbrush

All-purpose white glue

Two 8½-inch (21.6cm) × 11-inch (27.9cm) sheets of sheet moss

Wire cutters

Medium-gauge wire

Pliers

General-purpose scissors

1.

Squeeze or pour a small amount of white acrylic paint onto a piece of waxed paper. Dab the sponge into the paint, then lightly blot the outside of the terra-cotta pot to create an antiqued look; let the pot dry completely.

2.

Use the serrated knife to sculpt one foam sphere to fit the pot snugly.

3.

Impale the second foam sphere on the stick, pressing a narrow collar of adhesive clay underneath the foam sphere to secure it.

4.

Use the paintbrush to lightly coat the outside of the sphere with white glue. Cover the sphere with sheet moss. Gently squeeze the sphere with both hands to secure the moss. Let the sphere dry thoroughly.

5.

To make small florist's staples, use the wire cutters to cut 1-inch (2.5cm) lengths of medium-gauge wire; then bend them into horseshoe-shaped staples (see "Making Your Own Florist's Staples" on page 37). Use the florist's staples to tack the sheet moss to the sphere where necessary.

6.

Use the scissors to cut a disk of sheet moss to cover the foam in the base of the container. Tuck in any raw edges between the pot and foam.

GOLDEN FLOWER GLOBE WITH A MOSS STEM

Instead of the roses used in Tea Roses on a Golden Stem on page 64, this topiary uses safflowers, strawflowers, and statice. The stem is played up by decorating it with moss, another design idea that can be taken in many other directions. Instead of covering the stem with moss, ribbon can be wound around the stem for a more festive look, while silk cord or braid could be used to attain an elegant effect. The stem could also be painted to coordinate with or offset the color of the flowers.

Finished Size: 19 inches (48.3cm) high, 10 inches (25.4cm) wide

You Will Need:

Dry-foam block, 9 inches (22.9cm) long × 4 inches (10.2cm) wide × 3 inches (7.6cm) high

Glazed terra-cotta pot, 4 inches (10.2cm) high, with a 4½-inch (11.4cm) diameter opening

Serrated knife

Dry-foam sphere, 6 inches (15.2cm) in diameter

18-inch (45.7cm) long dowel, ½ inch (1.3cm) in diameter

Adhesive clay (florist's clay tape)

Florist's scissors

32 stems of yellow statice

24 yellow strawflowers

12 gold strawflowers

8 orange safflowers

12 small rust silk leaves

5 ounces (140g) of reindeer moss

1.

Press one side of the foam block onto the rim of the pot to make an indentation in the foam.

2.

Using the indentation mark as a guide, use the serrated knife to sculpt the foam block to fit snugly inside the pot.

3.

Impale the foam sphere on the dowel, pressing a collar of adhesive clay around the dowel just under the foam to secure it.

4.

Use the florist's scissors to trim the stems of all dried material to 3 inches (7.6cm).

5.

Beginning with the largest varieties and working down to the smallest, insert the flowers into the foam, making sure that the flower heads radiate outward and are distributed evenly around the sphere.

6.

To finish, insert the stems of the silk leaves as an accent.

7.

Conceal the dowel and foam in the container with moss, securing it with strips of adhesive clay.

SEA LAVENDER WITH TEA ROSES

Sea lavender is a frothy flower that grows in arched sprays with multiple buds. It makes an excellent filler material, but its rough, sharp stems and flowers necessitate wearing gloves when working with it. The main stems also contain so many flowering branches that it is often necessary to cut smaller sections from the main stem in order to work more easily with the plant.

The design featured here appears airy and light, but is actually quite top-heavy due to the abundance of dried material inserted into the topiary head. In order to counterbalance the weight of the topiary head, it is necessary to prepare a weighted container using plaster of paris.

Finished Size: 22 inches (55.9cm) high, 14 inches (35.6cm) wide

You Will Need:

Saber saw

17-inch (43.2cm) long dowel, $\frac{1}{2}$ inch (1.3cm) in diameter

6–8 wedges of dry foam, each approximately 4 inches (10.2cm) long × 1 inch (2.5cm) wide

2 terra-cotta pots: one outer pot, 4 inches (10.2cm) high, with a 6-inch (15.2cm) diameter opening; one inner pot, 4 inches (10.2cm) high, with a 4$\frac{1}{2}$-inch (11.4cm) diameter opening

Plaster of paris

Plastic mixing bowl

Wooden paint stirrer

Dry-foam sphere, 6 inches (15.2cm) in diameter

Adhesive clay (florist's clay tape)

General-purpose scissors

Packing tape

Florist's scissors

32 branches of sea lavender

48 pink tea roses

12 ounces (336g) of reindeer moss

1.

Prepare the smaller terra-cotta pot following directions for "Constructing the Basic Globe Topiary with a Weighted Container" on page 42.

2.

Use the florist's scissors to trim the stems of sea lavender to approximately 5 inches (12.7cm). (Because sea lavender grows in cascading arches, your cutting will be uneven. The effect will add beauty to the arrangement.)

3.

Insert the stems of sea lavender all over the sphere, making certain that the flowers radiate outward. Pierce taped areas with the point of the scissors before inserting the dried material. (You will have to brace the back of the topiary head with one hand as you work around the sphere inserting the dried material with the other hand.)

4.

Trim the rose stems to 6 inches (15.2cm), then insert them throughout the arrangement as shown.

5.

To display, place the finished topiary into the larger pot. Conceal the foam in the container with mounds of reindeer moss.

SEA LAVENDER WITH A MULTISTEM TRUNK

Concealing a stem made from a dowel not only makes this topiary more attractive, but also creates textural interest. Precut lengths of grapevine (chosen for its undulating nature) were bound to the supporting dowel stem with wire. Other materials, such as sphagnum or sheet moss, or wheat, can also be used to conceal the supporting dowel and enhance the impact of the topiary.

Another reason to decorate the stem is that you can use it to highlight other components of the topiary. If a topiary contains roses, for example, you can wrap the stem with rose stems (with or without the flowers). Another option is to arrange lengths of leafy branches around the supporting dowel, tying them in place with raffia. Each of these coverings presents a distinct decorating style: the roses might go with a more formal topiary, while the leafy branches might be compatible with a more rustic topiary.

Finished Size: 22 inches (55.9cm) high, 14 inches (35.6cm) wide

You Will Need:

Metal urn with a flared top, 6½ inches (16.5cm) high, with a 5-inch (12.7cm) square opening

1 pound (454g) of florist's clay

17-inch (43.2cm) long dowel, ¼ inch (0.6cm) in diameter

Four 6-inch (15.2cm) to 7-inch (17.8cm) lengths of straight grapevine or curly willow

Brass spool wire

Wire cutters

Styrofoam sphere, 6 inches (15.2cm) in diameter

Adhesive clay (florist's clay tape)

Packing tape

General-purpose scissors

Florist's scissors

30 stems of sea lavender

5 ounces (140g) of reindeer moss

1.

Fill the urn with florist's clay. Insert the dowel into the center of the clay, pushing it straight down until it touches the bottom of the urn.

2.

Conceal the dowel with lengths of straight grapevine or curly willow, leaving the top 5½ inches (14cm) of the dowel undecorated to accommodate the foam sphere. Cut lengths of brass spool wire and use the wire to secure the grapevine or willow at the top and bottom of the dowel.

3.

Center and impale the foam sphere on the dowel, pushing straight down until the sphere touches the vine wrapping. Secure the sphere with a collar of adhesive clay. Crisscross two lengths of packing tape over the top of the sphere; wind the loose ends around the dowel, just beneath the sphere.

4.

Use the florist's scissors to cut the sea lavender into 3-inch (7.6cm) stems. Insert the stems of sea lavender all over the sphere, making certain that the flowers radiate outward. Pierce taped areas with the point of the scissors before inserting the dried material. You will have to brace the back of the topiary head with one hand as you work around the sphere inserting the dried material with the other hand.

5.

Conceal the clay in the container with buns of reindeer moss.

BOXWOOD AND STATICE GLOBES

This design uses two foam spheres instead of one. Although shown here in a relatively small scale, this same construction principle can be applied to larger arrangements for a more formal statement. Instead of decorating each of the spheres with foliage and then adding floral accents, you could try decorating the spheres with flowers only; the impact is lovely. Purple statice on both spheres is pretty, as are white strawflowers accented by bands of deep red roses.

Finished Size: 18 inches (45.7cm) high, 6 inches (15.2cm) wide

You Will Need:

Glazed china teapot, 5½ inches (14cm) high with a 3½-inch (8.9cm) diameter opening (Do not use a valuable pot. Florist's clay is difficult to remove without the risk of breaking the pot.)

1 pound (454g) of florist's clay

16-inch (40.6cm) long dowel, ¼ inch (0.6cm) in diameter

Two dry-foam spheres, 4 inches (10.2cm) in diameter

Adhesive clay (florist's clay tape)

Pruning shears

16 branches of boxwood, painted green

Florist's scissors

16 stems of white statice

1.

To weight the teapot, fill the pot with wads of florist's clay to just below the rim.

2.

Center and insert the dowel into the clay.

3.

Impale one foam sphere on the dowel and push it down to 4 inches (10.2cm) above the rim of the pot. Secure it with a collar of adhesive clay.

4.

Use the pruning shears to trim the boxwood branches to 2½-inch (6.4cm) lengths.

5.

Insert the boxwood in the foam sphere with the branches radiating outward; cover the sphere completely.

6.

Impale the second foam sphere on the dowel and push it down to 4 inches (10.2cm) above the decorated sphere.

7.

Cover the top sphere completely with boxwood as described in Step 5.

8.

Push the top sphere down to abut the bottom decorated sphere.

9.

Use the florist's scissors to trim the statice to 3-inch (7.6cm) lengths. Referring to the photograph, insert the stems in an even pattern among the boxwood on both spheres.

Chapter 7

THE STANDARD TOPIARY

LAVENDER IN AN ANTIQUED POT

Lavender is a good material for a first standard topiary, as it is very easy to work with: its stems are straight and strong, and its buds are uniform and sturdy. With such cooperative elements, good results are practically guaranteed.

Finished Size: 15 inches (38.1cm) high, 4½ inches (11.4cm) wide

You Will Need:

White acrylic paint

Waxed paper

Household sponge

Terra-cotta pot, 3 inches (7.6cm) high, with a 3½-inch (8.9cm) diameter opening

Serrated knife

Dry-foam block, 9 inches (22.8cm) long × 4 inches (10cm) wide × 3 inches (7.6cm) high

80 stems of lavender

General-purpose scissors

Nylon string

Cotton ball

Vial of lavender oil

½ yard (45.7cm) of copper wire-edged ribbon, ½ inch (1.3cm) wide

4-inch (10.2cm) square of sheet moss

1.

Squeeze or pour the white acrylic paint onto a piece of waxed paper. Dab the sponge into the paint, then lightly blot the outside of the terra-cotta pot to create an antiqued look; let it dry completely.

2.

Use the serrated knife to sculpt the dry foam to fit snugly inside the pot.

3.

Lay the stems of the lavender on a flat work surface and trim the ends even with scissors.

4.

Gather the stems together, aligning the lavender heads in a spray; bind the bouquet 1 inch (2.5cm) below the lavender heads with the string.

5.

To add fragrance to the arrangement, dab a cotton ball in the lavender oil. Tuck the cotton ball inside the stem bunch, then use the string to bind the stems together approximately 2½ inches (6.4cm) above the ends.

6.

Hold the bouquet in two hands and push the stems into the foam in the container using steady, even pressure until the bouquet can stand alone (approximately 2 inches [5.1cm] deep).

7.

Conceal the string with a length of ribbon twisted and tied in a neat knot at the back of the arrangement. Conceal the foam with a piece of sheet moss trimmed to size.

DRIED VEGETABLES IN A WOODEN TRUG

There is no "order" to speak of in this arrangement, for it is simply based upon creating a pleasing juxtaposition of color and texture. The design, however, is unified by the muted palette, one that calls the viewer in to get a closer look at the curly edged cabbage leaves tinged with purple and green, and to discover the soft pink rosebuds nestled between the spiky safflowers.

This particular design is easy to make up, and its principle of construction, to create a sense of lush abundance, is applicable to any small box or basket. Wood or cardboard Shaker-style boxes, metal tins, china bowls with colorful patterns, old wooden drawers, and trays with low sides are just a few of the possible options.

Finished Size: 11 inches (27.9cm) high × 13½ inches (34.3cm) wide × 6 inches (15.2cm) deep

You Will Need:

2 dry-foam blocks, 9 inches (22.9cm) long × 4 inches (10.2cm) wide × 3 inches (7.6cm) high

Wooden trug stained white, 5½ inches (14cm) high × 13½ inches (34.3cm) wide × 6 inches (15.2cm) deep

Adhesive clay (florist's clay tape)

Serrated knife

4 artichokes

3 commercially dried purple and green cabbages

Hot glue gun and glue sticks

2 sunflower heads

12 bleached poppyheads

10 cream tea roses with peach-edged petals

10 pink tea roses

10 safflower buds

8 stems of love-lies-bleeding, dyed light green

12 sprigs of light green silk berries

½ yard (45.7cm) of dark green wire-edged ribbon, ½ inch (1.3cm) wide

Florist's pick

1.

Insert one block of dry foam inside the trug, securing it at the bottom with a strip of adhesive clay.

2.

Press the second block of dry foam in its intended position to create an indentation mark. Using this mark as a guide, sculpt the foam with a serrated knife so that it fits snugly inside the container next to the first laid section of foam. Make certain that the foam blocks cover the trug bottom and are even with the rim of the container.

3.

Insert the stems of the artichokes in the top center of the foam. Surround the artichokes with the cabbages, securing them with hot glue if the stems are not long enough to anchor the material.

4.

Use the photograph as a guide to adding other materials, inserting stems or hot-gluing elements in a spray radiating outward.

5.

Accent the arrangement with a ribbon tied in a bow and secured with a florist's pick.

RYE WITH BERRIES

Grasses such as rye or wheat are well suited to dried-flower topiaries. Like lavender, rye and wheat are easy to work with because of their sturdy stalks and grainy heads.

As you work with rye, you'll notice that adding stalks to the bouquet causes the rye to flare. Flaring is a desirable effect since it creates an attractive contour and adds textural interest to what would otherwise be a plain arrangement.

For variations, you could use other straight-stemmed plant material such as lavender, German statice, or phalaris. You could also make a topiary with shorter lengths of grass for a different look. Should you do this, you'll want to use a smaller pot in order to keep the design in proportion.

Finished Size: 24 inches (61cm) high, 5½ inches (14cm) wide

You Will Need:

Serrated knife

Dry-foam block, 9 inches (22.9cm) long × 4 inches (10.2cm) wide × 3 inches (7.6cm) high

Metal urn with a flared top, 6½ inches (16.5cm) high, with a 5-inch (12.7cm) square opening

100 stems of rye

Florist's scissors

Nylon string

Silk berries on wire

5-inch (12.7cm) square of sheet moss

1.

Use the knife to sculpt the dry foam to fit snugly inside the urn.

2.

Lay the stems of rye on a flat work surface and trim the ends even with scissors.

3.

Gather the stems together, aligning the rye heads in a spray; bind the bouquet 1 inch (2.5cm) below the rye heads with the string.

4.

Hold the bouquet in two hands and push the stems into the foam in the container using steady, even pressure until the bouquet can stand alone (approximately 2 inches [5.1cm] deep).

5.

Wind silk berries around the bouquet to conceal the string.

6.

Conceal the foam with sheet moss.

WALL BOUQUET

The standard topiary is typically associated with orderly rows of dried material, but this particular arrangement breaks the rules—with beautiful results. Wild grass and flowers are gathered into a bouquet, tied with raffia, then displayed on the wall. The stems of the flowers are cut to accommodate the design of the bouquet; then the flowers are laid down. Textural variety is an important consideration as it adds visual interest: mix spiky flowers with rounder blooms, smooth textures with rough ones.

Because this bouquet is so easy to make and can be composed quickly, you can readily make small arrangements as studies for larger works.

Finished Size: 25 inches (63.5cm) high, 16 inches (40.6cm) wide

You will need:

8 branches of melaleuca foliage (or eucalyptus)

30 blades of isoplexis (or any long-blade grass)

24 stems of larkspur

60–70 stems of red phalaris

40 stems of chamomile, dyed blue

40 stems of chamomile, dyed red

Nylon string

Hank of raffia strands, ¾ inch (1.9cm) in diameter

Display hook

1.

On a flat worktable, lay a bed of foliage and grass so that the stems line up evenly.

2.

Layer one type of flower on top of the foliage, so that the heads are slightly lower than the tallest foliage.

3.

Continue adding layers of flowers in this manner until all the flowers have been used.

4.

Gather the foliage and flowers in a bouquet, covering the front stems with more foliage. Bind the bouquet together with string.

5.

Tie a rope of raffia around the bouquet to conceal the string, twisting the raffia slightly to prevent the short ends from sticking out. Tie the raffia in a large double knot; trim the ends even as shown.

6.

Tie a string in a long loop at the back of the bouquet. To display, hang the bouquet from a hook.

Bands of Flowers in a Painted Trug

The impact of this standard-style arrangement is intensified by strong color contrasts, such as the purple phalaris and the golden yarrow, and the blue trug and the deep rose cockscomb. You can readily adapt this design to any flowers you wish to use: try more subtle mixes, such as pastels, or monochromatic arrangements, such as a blend of flowers, pods, and leaves in natural tones.

Finished Size: 8½ inches (21.6cm) high × 12½ inches (31.8cm) wide × 6½ inches (16.5cm) deep

You Will Need:

2 dry-foam blocks, 9 inches (22.9cm) long × 4 inches (10.2cm) wide × 3 inches (7.6cm) high

Trug painted blue, 6 inches (15.2cm) high × 12 inches (30.5cm) wide × 6 inches (15.2cm) deep

Adhesive clay (florist's clay tape)

Serrated knife

Florist's scissors

24 stalks of deep rose cockscomb

74 purple phalaris

24 stalks of cream cockscomb

34 magenta tea roses

24 stems of golden yarrow

Ruler and pencil

1.

To prepare the trug, follow Steps 1 and 2 of Dried Vegetables in a Wooden Trug on page 87.

2.

Use the florist's scissors to trim all the stems to 5 inches (12.7cm).

3.

Use the ruler and pencil to mark off 7 equal bands in the foam.

4.

Referring to the photograph, decorate the arrangement as follows: insert a row of deep rose cockscomb in the center band, followed by two even and adjacent bands of purple phalaris. Add cream cockscomb, then magenta tea roses in equal bands. Finish with bands of golden yarrow.

5.

Fill in any bare spots in the bands with like flowers.

THREE-TIERED WHEAT AND ROSES STANDARD

This topiary is a simple variation on Rye with Berries on page 88. A collar of roses and a collar of wheat are added to the central stand of wheat. The result is a sophisticated topiary—without a lot of work.

Finished Size: 22 inches (55.9cm) high, 8 inches (20.3cm) wide

You Will Need:

Serrated knife

Dry-foam block, 9 inches (22.9cm) long × 4 inches (10.2cm) wide × 3 inches (7.6cm) high

Container, 5 inches (12.7cm) high, with a 5½-inch (14cm) diameter opening

100 stems of triticum wheat

Florist's scissors

Nylon string

Silk berries on wire

24 pink tea roses with 12-inch (30.5cm) stems

8-strand raffia hank, 18 inches (45.7cm) long

6 stems of golden yarrow

1.

Follow Steps 1–5 for Rye with Berries on page 88; substitute 60 stems of wheat for the rye.

2.

Trim the rose stems to 11 inches (27.9cm) and insert them around the central standard of wheat.

3.

Trim the remaining 40 stems of wheat to 8 inches (20.3cm) and insert the stems in a collar around the rose stems.

4.

Tie the raffia rope around the standard.

5.

Trim the stems of the yarrow to 2 inches (5.1cm). Insert the yarrow in a collar around the base of the standard.

Chapter 8

TOPIARY VARIATIONS

MOSS CONE IN A CHINA POT

Simple to make, this topiary is a moss-covered cone around which is glued a rope made of the same moss. A variation on the globe topiary, the arrangement was inspired by the hedge sculptures of sixteenth- and seventeenth-century gardens. Conical shapes were popular at this time, as were the diamond, oval, and combinations thereof. Each topiary was scrupulously maintained, and resident gardeners spent much time shaping the unruly branches into ornamental forms including beasts, crests, arches, and gates, in addition to geometrically based structures.

Finished Size: 8½ inches (21.6cm) high, 4½-inch (11.4cm) diameter at base

You Will Need:

Serrated knife

Dry-foam block, 9 inches (22.9cm) long × 4 inches (10.2cm) wide × 3 inches (7.6cm) high

Glazed china pot, 3 inches (7.6cm) high with a 3½-inch (8.9cm) diameter opening

6-inch (15.2cm) long dowel, ¼ inch (0.6cm) in diameter

Small paintbrush

White glue

12 ounces (336g) of reindeer moss

Dry-foam cone, 4½ inches (11.4cm) high, 4-inch (10.2cm) diameter at base

Florist's staples with 1½-inch (3.8cm) legs (See page 39 for "Making Your Own Florist's Staples.")

Green thread

1.

Use the serrated knife to sculpt the dry-foam block to fit snugly inside the pot.

2.

Center and insert the dowel in the foam in the container.

3.

Use the paintbrush to cover the cone lightly with white glue. Wind the reindeer moss into small buns; then cover the entire outer surface of the cone (excluding the underside) with the moss buns. Bind the moss in place with florist's staples.

4.

Make a 28-inch (71.1cm) rope of moss: overlap sections of moss and bind them together at each joint with thread.

5.

Center and impale the moss-covered cone on the dowel.

6.

Working from top to bottom, wind the moss rope around the cone; secure it with florist's staples.

FINIAL OF GREEN AND GOLD LEAVES

In this arrangement, a variation on the dome topiary, a simple dry-foam cone is layered with green and gold leaves, but it would be equally attractive to attach the tiers of leaves to other shapes such as orbs, obelisks, and cubes. The simple flat leaves make the layering process neat and easy.

Finished Size: 10 inches (25.4cm) high, 5½-inch (14cm) diameter at base

You Will Need:

20 lemon leaves or salal painted gold (or follow Step 1 to paint your own leaves)

Newspaper

Gold spray paint

Dry-foam cone, 10 inches (25.4cm) high, 5½-inch (14cm) diameter at base

40 white mallee eucalyptus leaves

Florist's staples

½ yard (45.7cm) of dark green wire-edged ribbon, 1 inch (2.5cm) wide

1.

Prepare gold leaves if necessary: lay the lemon leaves or salal on newspaper and spray paint one side gold. When they are dry, turn the leaves over and spray paint the other side. Let the leaves dry completely.

2.

Working from top to bottom, decorate the cone with leaves: position 1 eucalyptus leaf near the top of the cone and secure it with 2 florist's staples at the bottom of the leaf (the staples will be concealed by the next layer of leaves). Place the next leaf so that it slightly overlaps a side of the first leaf; then secure it with 2 florist's staples.

3.

Working in rounds, position and staple the eucalyptus leaves in place to cover the top ⅔ of the cone. Be sure to conceal the leaf bottoms of each row with the leaf tips of the new row.

4.

Cover the bottom ⅓ of the cone with 2 rounds of gold leaves.

5.

Tie a ribbon bow around the base of the finial for an accent.

MOSS CONE AND SPHERE

A simple variation of Sheet Moss in an Antiqued Pot on page 67, this topiary design puts together a moss-covered cone and sphere to re-create the look of an early English hedge garden.

Finished Size: 16 inches (40.6cm) high, 6 inches (15.2cm) wide

You Will Need:

Terra-cotta pot, 5 inches (12.7cm) high with a 5-inch (12.7cm) diameter opening

1 pound (454g) of florist's clay

17-inch (43.2cm) long dowel, ¼ inch (0.6cm) in diameter

Small paintbrush

White glue

White Styrofoam sphere, 4 inches (10.2cm) in diameter

White Styrofoam cone, 4-inch (10.2cm) diameter at base

Three 8½-inch (21.6cm) × 11-inch (27.9cm) sheets of sheet moss

Florist's staples

Skewer

Green thread

Florist's scissors

24 stems of red chamomile

1.

To weight the pot, fill it with wads of florist's clay to just below the rim.

2.

Center and insert the dowel into the clay.

3.

Use the paintbrush to apply a thin coat of white glue on each foam shape. Cover the foam sphere and cone with sheet moss, securing the foam with florist's staples.

4.

Use the skewer to poke a "starter" hole through the moss-covered sphere; then impale the sphere on the dowel, pushing straight down with even pressure.

5.

Repeat Step 3 for the cone, pushing it down on the dowel until the base of the cone touches the sphere. Wrap the cone and sphere at even intervals with green thread to secure the moss.

6.

Use the florist's scissors to trim the chamomile stems to 2 inches (5.1cm). Referring to the photograph, insert the chamomile into the sphere and cone, using even pressure to push the stems through the outer covering of moss. (If a stem breaks, glue the flower head in place.)

7.

Conceal the florist's clay with sheet moss trimmed to size.

HERB CONE WITH A MINIATURE ROSE BASE

A pretty, decorative accent, this topiary uses culinary herbs. Oregano is featured here, but other herbs, such as sage or bay leaf, could be substituted for an equally attractive result. A larger cone-shaped head would enable you to decorate the topiary with dried chili peppers, garlic, and the like; all you need is a larger container to maintain the correct proportions.

Finished Size: 10½ inches (26.7cm) high, 4-inch (10.2cm) diameter at base

You Will Need:

Terra-cotta pot, 3 inches (7.6cm) high, with a 3¼-inch (8.3cm) diameter opening

Adhesive clay (florist's clay tape)

Dry-foam sphere, 3 inches (7.6cm) in diameter

Hot glue gun and glue sticks

100 miniature pink rosebuds

8-inch (20.3cm) long dowel, ¼ inch (0.6cm) in diameter

Florist's scissors

6–8 rose stems (without flowers)

Dry-foam cone, 4 inches (10.2cm) high, 3½-inch (8.9cm) diameter at base

12 stems of oregano

Brass spool wire

Wire cutters

1.

Follow the directions for making Miniature Rosebuds in a Terra-Cotta Pot on page 50, but do not finish gluing rosebuds in the top center of the dome. Instead, center and insert the dowel in the top center of the dome.

2.

Use the florist's scissors to trim the rose stems to approximately 2 inches (5.1cm) and hot-glue them around the dowel.

3.

Continue hot-gluing rosebuds in a tight row or two to form a collar around the stems at the center of the dome.

4.

Center and impale the foam cone on the dowel, pushing it down to meet the stem-wrapped trunk.

5.

Trim the oregano stems to 2½ inches (6.4cm). Use the wire cutters to cut the brass spool wire; then wire bunches consisting of 4 to 6 stems of oregano.

6.

Hot-glue the oregano bunches to the foam cone in order to cover it completely.

FRUIT AND FLOWERS WITH ROSE STEMS

A variation on Sea Lavender with a Multistem Trunk on page 76, this topiary style utilizes rose stems that were not used in another topiary, but here serve to conceal the plain wood of the supporting dowel. The large globe head is decorated with an abundance of dried flowers to create a contrast of textures and colors. Silk berries and grapes and dried orange slices add interesting accents.

Finished Size: 20 inches (50.8cm) high, 13 inches (33cm) in diameter

You Will Need:

Saber saw

18-inch (45.7cm) long dowel, ½ inch (1.3cm) in diameter

8 wedges of dry foam, approximately 5 inches (12.7cm) long

Terra-cotta pot, 5½ inches (14cm) high, with a 6-inch (15.2cm) diameter opening

Plaster of paris

Plastic mixing bowl

Wooden paint stirrer

Styrofoam sphere, 6 inches (15.2cm) in diameter

Adhesive clay (florist's clay tape)

General-purpose scissors

Packing tape

Medium-gauge wire

Florist's scissors

8 pink tea roses with 10-inch (25.4cm) stems

Wire cutters

Brass spool wire

10 stems of sea lavender

4 stalks of deep pink cockscomb

4 stalks of cream cockscomb

10 blue mop-headed hydrangea

3 yellow tansy

6 golden yarrow

6 white strawflowers

6 yellow strawflowers

4 gold strawflowers

10 blue salvia

4 orange slices (purchase commercially dried orange slices, or dry your own on chicken wire; see the directions on page 25)

4 small silk grape clusters

6 clusters of gold silk berries

6-inch (15.2cm) disk of sheet moss

1.

Follow the directions for "Constructing the Basic Globe Topiary with a Weighted Container" on page 42. Wire any elements without stems or in need of reinforcement following the directions in Chapter 3, "Preparing Plant Material."

2.

Use the florist's scissors to cut the rose heads from their stems 4½ inches (11.4cm) below the head. Set the rose heads aside.

3.

Conceal the dowel with rose stems. Use the wire cutters to cut lengths of brass wire; then secure the rose stems to the base and midpoint of the dowel.

4.

Trim the stems of the sea lavender to 4½ inches (11.4cm) and insert them in the foam in a soft spray pattern.

5.

Insert the remaining dried materials: beginning with the largest pieces and working down to the smallest, insert one type of material at a time, distributing the stems evenly on the topiary head.

6.

Fill in any bare areas with hydrangea florets.

7.

Conceal the plaster with sheet moss trimmed to size.

Heart-Shaped Topiary

This heart-shaped topiary puts to use a great variety of dried material and is a terrific way to utilize broken flower heads and sprigs left over from other projects. The mix of delicate pastel blooms along with the open heart-shaped topiary head lends the arrangement a very romantic touch. If you prefer, an open circle, or any free-form shape, could take the place of the heart. The only technical difference would be substituting an appropriately shaped metal frame for the one used here.

Finished Size: 14 inches (35.6cm) high, 8 inches (20.3cm) wide

You Will Need:

Saber saw

5-inch (12.7cm) long dowel, ½ inch (1.3cm) in diameter

4–5 dry-foam wedges, 4 inches (10.2cm) long × 1 inch (2.5cm) wide

Terra-cotta pot, 5 inches (12.7cm) high, with a 5½-inch (14cm) diameter opening

Plaster of paris

Plastic mixing bowl

Wooden paint stirrer

Wire cutters

Wire clothes hanger

Pliers

Medium-gauge spool wire

Heart-shaped wire frame, 8 inches (20.3cm) high

Green thread

2 to 3 ounces (56–85g) of sphagnum moss

Hot glue gun and glue sticks

48 pink tea roses

60 miniature rosebuds

20 pink strawflowers

20 white strawflowers

Sprigs of sea lavender, larkspur, golden yarrow, purple statice, yellow statice, and boxwood

Two 8½-inch (21.6cm) × 11-inch (27.9cm) sheets of sheet moss

1.

Follow Steps 1–5 in the directions for "Constructing the Basic Globe Topiary with a Weighted Container" on pages 42–43.

2.

Use the wire cutters to cut the crossbar off the wire hanger so that the hook and two arms remain; use the pliers to bend the hook straight.

3.

Use the spool wire to bind the straightened hook to the center of the dowel.

4.

Bend the arms in a V and attach them to the V of the heart frame using spool wire; make certain that the heart frame is secure.

5.

Use thread to bind wads of sphagnum moss to the heart frame.

6.

Hot-glue flowers in a colorful variety to all surfaces of the moss-covered heart; finish with sprig accents.

7.

Conceal the plaster in the pot with sheet moss trimmed to size.

MAYPOLE WREATH

This variation on the globe topiary, because of the use of a dowel, was also inspired by the open nature of the Heart-Shaped Topiary on page 109. Suspended from the stem with white ribbons, this innovative topiary head features delicate blossoms in white and blue. White ribbon streamers top the stem in maypole fashion to complete the design's airy spring look.

Finished Size: 22 inches (55.9cm) high, 18 inches (45.7cm) wide

You Will Need:

Saber saw

22-inch (55.9cm) long dowel, ¾ inch (1.9cm) in diameter

6–8 dry-foam wedges, approximately 4 inches (10.2cm) long × 1 inch (2.5cm) wide

Terra-cotta pot, 5 inches (12.7cm) high, 5½ inches (14cm) in diameter

Container, 12 inches (30.5cm) high, with a 12-inch (30.5cm) outer diameter

Plaster of paris

Wooden paint stirrer

Plastic mixing bowl

Straw wreath, 16 inches (40.6cm) in diameter

8 ounces (227g) of sphagnum moss

Green heavyweight thread

Florist's scissors

24 white strawflowers

10 white silk roses

16 stems of purple larkspur

12 stems of light green love-lies-bleeding

40 stems of chamomile, dyed blue

6 stems of purple statice

6 stems of golden yarrow

Hot glue gun and glue sticks

4 yards (43.8m) of white satin ribbon, ¾ inch (1.9cm) wide

Wire cutters

Brass spool wire

Container, 12 inches (30.5cm) high, with a 12-inch (30.5cm) outer diameter

Two 8½-inch (21.6cm) × 11-inch (27.9cm) sheets of sheet moss

1.

Follow Steps 1–5 in the directions for "Constructing the Basic Globe Topiary with a Weighted Container" on pages 42–43 for the terra-cotta pot.

2.

Prepare the wreath for decoration by binding overlapping wads of sphagnum moss on all surfaces of the wreath using heavyweight thread.

3.

Use the florist's scissors to trim all stems to 4 inches (10.2cm).

4.

Hot-glue the dried and silk floral materials around the wreath, starting with the largest pieces and working down to the smallest. Work with one type of floral material at a time and distribute it evenly. Alternate heights of adjacent flowers and foliage to create an airy effect.

5.

Wind the ribbon around the center dowel, securing it with dabs of hot glue; cut the ribbon when the dowel is covered.

6.

Lay a 1-yard (91.4cm) length of ribbon horizontally across the center of the wreath; wrap the loose ends around the wreath and tie them in a knot at each side to secure. Repeat with another 1-yard (91.4cm) length of ribbon, laying it over the wreath vertically.

7.

Cut an 8-inch (20.3cm) length of ribbon and tie it at the intersection of the ribbons to secure.

8.

Referring to the photograph, balance the intersection of ribbons on the dowel and bind it tightly in place with wire.

9.

Place the arrangement in a larger decorative container. Finish by adding streamers and bows as desired.

10.

Conceal the plaster in the pot with sheet moss trimmed to size.

APPENDICES

CARING FOR DRIED-FLOWER TOPIARIES

Do not move topiaries frequently or vigorously. Dried-flower topiaries should be handled gently, as their dried petals and leaves are intrinsically fragile. Moving the topiary frequently from one location to another increases the risk of its being bumped and broken, so try to select a safer, more permanent setting for display, such as a mantel, shelf, table, or cold hearth. If you must move a topiary, hold the container from underneath and keep the weight of the head equally distributed as you carry the arrangement to its new location.

Do not expose topiaries to direct sunlight. Subject to fading, dried materials should be kept out of direct sunlight. A room with northern or southern exposure is best, as it gets indirect light. If direct light is unavoidable, a curtain or shade can help to retard bleaching. Never display a topiary outside in the sun or leave it outdoors.

Keep topiaries in a cool, dry environment. Excessive humidity will cause petals and leaves to soften and droop. This is why you should avoid displaying or storing dried-flower arrangements in a bathroom or kitchen.

If humidity is a real problem where you live, you may wish to use a dehumidifier or store your topiary in an airtight container, such as a plastic garbage can or large biscuit tin, and display it in drier months. To prepare an airtight container, simply place a few inches of silica gel on the bottom of the container that is large enough to hold the entire construction and place the topiary inside. Close the container lid and secure it with masking tape. Store the container in a cool, dry, dimly lit place until you are ready to display the topiary again.

Cleaning and Repairing Dried-Flower Topiaries

It is natural for a topiary to suffer some breakage and fading, but here are a few suggestions for keeping arrangements in top condition.

To remove dust from flowers and foliage, gently brush the bristles of a soft artist's paintbrush over the surface of each element. To remove dust on very delicate elements, dampen a cotton swab with a little water and dab gently.

The three most common topiary repairs are: replacing a flower head or leaf, creating a false stem or reinforcing a weak one, and rejuvenating the color of a faded arrangement.

You can reaffix or replace a broken flower head or leaf as follows. Gently grasp the stem with a pair of tweezers; then place a dab of hot glue on the blunt end of the stem underneath the flower or leaf stub. Hold everything in place until the glue sets up (this takes only a few seconds).

To create a false stem or to reinforce a weak one, refer to "Wiring and Wrapping Stems" on page 30.

Sometimes faded flowers and foliage are pretty in themselves, or make a nice contrasting backdrop for added material. To freshen a faded arrangement, add more vibrantly colored flowers by inserting the new plant material between the faded blooms or in specific patterns. You can also spray paint the entire construction with acrylic paint.

Finally, a dried-flower topiary may be too unattractive to display any longer. Simply remove the dried blooms from the container, keeping any salvageable materials. To reuse the container, clean it with a damp cloth. Pots that have been weighted with plaster of paris are reusable: just remove the head of the old topiary, snipping away any tape that held the foam in place. You can then position a new head on the dowel and redecorate it.

Most dry foam that has been pierced with stems or other sharp items is not reusable, as in the example of a globe topiary head that has broken off its stem. In this case, the foam head will need to be replaced, as the channel in the foam will no longer be snug enough to hug the dowel. It is possible, however, to reuse the foam topiary head for decorative material that doesn't need to be inserted. Simply wrap the foam with a cover material, such as sheet moss, and use hot glue to adhere the new decoration.

DRIED FLOWERS AND FOLIAGE USED IN THIS BOOK

LATIN NAME	COMMON NAME
Achillea sp.	Yarrow
Amaranthus caudatus	Love-lies-bleeding
Anthemis nobilis	Chamomile
Buxus sp.	Boxwood
Carthamus tinctorius	Safflower
Celosia cristata	Cockscomb
Cladonia rangiferina	Reindeer moss
Craspedia globosa	Craspedia
Cynara Scolymus	Globe artichoke
Delphinium Consolida	Larkspur
Eucalyptus sp.	Eucalyptus
Gaultheria Shallon	Salal, Lemon leaves
Helianthus sp.	Sunflower
Helichrysum bracteatum	Strawflower
Hydrangea macrophylla	French hydrangea
Ilex sp.	Holly
Isoplexis sp.	Isoplexis
Lavandula sp.	Lavender
Limonium sp.	Sea lavender
Limonium sinuatum	Statice
Melaleuca sp.	Melaleuca
Mnium sp.	Sheet moss
Myristica fragrans	Nutmeg
Nelumbo nucifera	Lotus pod
Origanum vulgare	Oregano
Papaver sp.	Poppy
Phalaris arundinacea	Phalaris
Pinus sp.	Pine (cones)
Rosa sp.	Rose
Salix Matsudana 'Tortuosa'	Curly willow, Corkscrew
Salvia azurea	Blue salvia
Secale sp.	Rye
Sphagnum sp.	Sphagnum moss
Tanacetum vulgare	Tansy
Triticum sp.	Wheat
Vitis sp.	Grapevine

Sources

The great appeal of making your own topiaries is that most of the necessary tools and materials are readily available from your local florist, hardware store, and craft store—not to mention your kitchen utensil drawer and toolbox. But here are some ideas of where to find the tools of the trade.

Tools and Materials

Pliers, wire cutters, saber saws, dowels, plaster of paris, nylon string, and spool wire can be found at your local hardware store. An inexpensive version of the saber saw designed for cutting dry foam is available at craft stores.

Pruning shears and florist's scissors can be found at most garden supply stores.

Chances are, you already own skewers, general-purpose and serrated knives, and general-purpose scissors. If not, these items can be found in the housewares section of most department stores and in some hardware stores.

Styrofoam, dry-foam (Oasis) blocks, planks, adhesive clay (florist's clay tape), cones, spheres, hot glue guns and glue sticks, florist's clay, stem wrap, and florist's staples and picks can be found at most craft stores and florist's supply shops.

Dried flowers, florist's scissors, spool wire, and stub wire are available in a wide variety at craft stores, at florist shops, and at some garden supply stores. Of course, dried flowers and foliage can be found in your own garden or can be "recycled" from fresh cut flowers that have peaked.

Containers can be found at department stores, at garden supply stores, and in gift and stationery shops. Check also for interesting finds at flea markets, garage sales, antique stores, and thrift shops.

Recommended Reading

Hillier, Malcolm, ed. *Flower Arranging*. New York: The Reader's Digest Association, Inc., 1990.

———, and Colin Hilton. *The Book of Dried Flowers*. New York: Simon and Schuster, 1986.

Packer, Jane. *Jane Packer's New Flower Arranging*. London: Trafalgar Square Publishing, 1994.

Tolley, Emelie, and Chris Meade. *Gifts From the Herb Garden*. New York: Clarkson Potter Publishers, 1991.

Turner, Kenneth. *Flower Style*. New York: Weidenfeld & Nicholson, 1989.

———. *The Floral Decorator*. New York: Random House, 1993.

INDEX